TIME
Annual 2012

YAHYA ARHAB—EPA

Digital message *As the Arab Spring movement swept the Middle East and North Africa, Yemeni women, fingers painted in the colors of the national flag, joined protests on March 11*

TIME

MANAGING EDITOR Richard Stengel
ART DIRECTOR D.W. Pine

Annual 2012

EDITOR Kelly Knauer
DESIGNER Ellen Fanning
PICTURE EDITOR Patricia Cadley
RESEARCH Tresa McBee
COPY EDITOR Bruce Christopher Carr

EDITORIAL DIRECTOR Stephen Koepp

TIME HOME ENTERTAINMENT
PUBLISHER Richard Fraiman
VICE PRESIDENT, BUSINESS DEVELOPMENT AND STRATEGY Steven Sandonato
EXECUTIVE DIRECTOR, MARKETING SERVICES Carol Pittard
EXECUTIVE DIRECTOR, RETAIL AND SPECIAL SALES Tom Mifsud
EXECUTIVE DIRECTOR, NEW PRODUCT DEVELOPMENT Peter Harper
DIRECTOR, BOOKAZINE DEVELOPMENT AND MARKETING Laura Adam
PUBLISHING DIRECTOR Joy Butts
FINANCE DIRECTOR Glenn Buonocore
ASSISTANT GENERAL COUNSEL Helen Wan
ASSISTANT DIRECTOR, SPECIAL SALES Ilene Schreider
BOOK PRODUCTION MANAGER Suzanne Janso
DESIGN AND PREPRESS MANAGER Anne-Michelle Gallero
BRAND MANAGER Michela Wilde
ASSOCIATE PREPRESS MANAGER Alex Voznesenskiy

SPECIAL THANKS TO:
Christine Austin, Jeremy Biloon, Jim Childs, Susan Chodakiewicz, Rose Cirrincione, Lauren Hall Clark, Brian Fellows, Jacqueline Fitzgerald, Christine Font, Jenna Goldberg, Carrie Hertan, Hillary Hirsch, Amy Mangus, Robert Marasco, Kimberly Marshall, Amy Migliaccio, Nina Mistry, Dave Rozzelle, Adriana Tierno, TIME Imaging, Vanessa Wu

ISBN 10: 1-60320-205-6
ISBN 13: 978-1-60320-205-3
ISSN: 1097-5721

Printed in the U.S.A.

Published by TIME Books, an imprint of Time Home Entertainment Inc.
135 W. 50th Street, New York, NY 10020

We welcome your comments and suggestions about TIME Books. Please write to us at:
TIME Books, Attention: Book Editors, P.O. Box 11016, Des Moines, IA 50336-1016

To order any of our hardcover Collector's Edition books, please call us at 1-800-327-6388.
Hours: Monday through Friday, 7 a.m.–8 p.m., or Saturday, 7 a.m.– 6 p.m., Central Time.

ROBERT STOLARIK—THE NEW YORK TIMES—REDUX

Face-off *New York City police confront protesters from the Occupy Wall Street movement on the Brooklyn Bridge on Oct. 1. More than 700 demonstrators from the burgeoning crusade were arrested*

SMASH PATRIARCHY SMASH CAPITALISM
WE THE PEOPLE
CAPITALISM IS ORGANIZED CRIME!
NYPD PROTECTS AND SERVES THE RICH.
WE ARE THE ONES WE HAVE BEEN WAITING FOR

Contents

Falling *The footprints of the Twin Towers at the World Trade Center in Manhattan, converted into waterfalls, are the heart of the new National September 11 Memorial and Museum*

POLARIS

LightBox

Protesters rally in the Wisconsin State Capitol on Feb. 25, during a showdown over the collective bargaining rights of public employees

SCOTT OLSON—GETTY IMAGES

3/11/11

Irresistible force
Tsunami waves sweep across the shore of the city of Iwanuma in Miyagi prefecture on Japan's northeast coast, swamping everything in their path. Triggered by an offshore earthquake, the year's most devastating disaster left as many as 20,000 people dead or missing and tens of thousands homeless

5/1/11

Watchful waiting

One of the year's most scrutinized photos showed only a roomful of people passively staring at a video screen. But the context charged the scene with high drama: President Barack Obama and his national security team are in the White House, following in real time the risky secret mission to find and kill al-Qaeda leader Osama bin Laden in Pakistan

PETER SOUZA—THE WHITE HOUSE VIA GETTY IMAGES

4/29/11

The sound and the fury
The world roared its approval as Britain's Prince William, second in line to the throne after his father Prince Charles, wed commoner Kate Middleton. At least one observer, bridal attendant Grace Van Cutsem, William's goddaughter, was not amused

MATT DUNHAM—AP IMAGES

2/2/11

Last gasp of the old order
As citizens of Arab nations in the Middle East and North Africa rose up to challenge authoritarian regimes, a supporter of Egypt's President, Hosni Mubarak, rides a camel into Cairo's Tahrir Square, center of the protests, in an attempt to break up a massive rally

MEHDI CHEBIL—POLARIS

11/23/11

Tail end of the story
U.S. soldiers, homeward-bound, board a C-130 transport plane at Baghdad airport. All U.S. combat troops were scheduled to depart Iraq by the end of 2011, fulfilling a 2008 campaign promise of Barack Obama's and ending a long, often frustrating chapter in the history of U.S. intervention abroad

SEBASTIAN MEYER—CORBIS

5/24/11

Wake of the storm

The powerful twister that struck Joplin, Mo., on May 22 was the deadliest tornado to hit the U.S. since 1947. Here, two days after the storm, a resident surveys the wide swath of wreckage churned up by its winds, which exceeded 200 m.p.h.

MARIO TAMA/GETTY IMAGES

10/16/11

Death on the oval

British driver Dan Wheldon, 33, a two-time Indianapolis 500 champion, was killed in the last IndyCar race of the season, at the Las Vegas Motor Speedway. Amid a horrific 15-car pileup, Wheldon's car, No. 77, went airborne, turned over and crashed into the fence above the retaining wall

ROBERT LABERGE—GETTY IMAGES

10/6/11

Gone Too Soon
The death of Apple Inc. co-founder Steve Jobs at only 56 provoked an outpouring of regard for the charismatic Silicon Valley innovator. Jobs' admirers stopped by an Apple store on Broadway in Manhattan to pay their respects at an impromptu memorial display

MARKUS HARTEL

Verbatim: Quotes of the Year

'When the Prime Minister came to Tahrir to speak to the people, was he blind? Did he not see that half of the people filling the square were women?'

NEHAD ABU EL KOMSAN, head of the Egyptian Center for Women's Rights, on the need for women to be included in Egypt's political process

'It's a legal product. I choose to smoke. Leave me alone.'

JOHN BOEHNER, Speaker of the House, after being asked about his tobacco habit

'They love me ... They will die to protect me, my people.'

MUAMMAR GADDAFI, Libyan dictator, denying the existence of protests against him, in March

'The damn show destroyed my family.'

BILLY RAY CYRUS, musician and actor, referring to the popular kids' television series *Hannah Montana,* which catapulted daughter Miley Cyrus to stardom

'I'd rather smoke crack than eat cheese from a can.'

GWYNETH PALTROW, actress and foodie, promoting her new cookbook on a British talk show; she did not offer her thoughts on crack from a can

'If you think about it, his perspective as growing up in Kenya with a Kenyan father and grandfather, their view of the Mau Mau revolution in Kenya is very different than ours.'

MIKE HUCKABEE, former Arkansas governor, stating incorrectly in a radio interview that President Obama grew up in Kenya; he later issued a statement saying he "misspoke" and "meant to say Indonesia," where the Hawaii-born Obama spent some childhood years

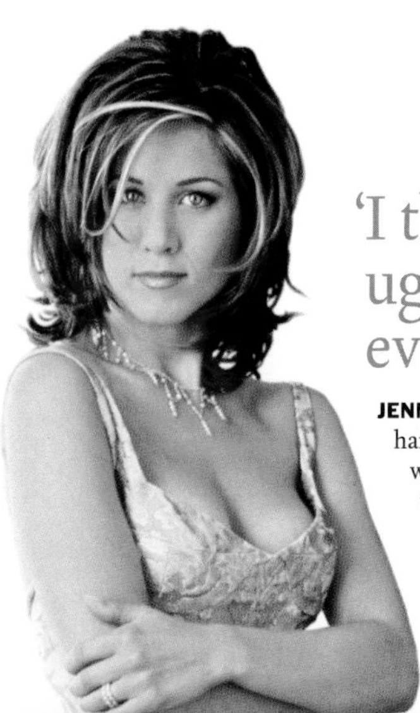

'I think it was the ugliest haircut I've ever seen.'

JENNIFER ANISTON, on the Rachel, a layered hairstyle—much mimicked by American women—made famous by the actress on the '90s hit sitcom *Friends*

TOP ROW, LEFT TO RIGHT: CARSTEN KOALL—GETTY IMAGES, TOM WILLIAMS—ROLL CALL—GETTY IMAGES, ABDEL MAGID AL FERGANY—AP IMAGES. MIDDLE: ERIC MCCANDLESS—DISNEY CHANNEL VIA GETTY IMAGES; ALBERTO PIZZOLI—AFP—GETTY IMAGES. BOTTOM: NBC—ONLINE VIA GETTY IMAGES; SAYYID AZIM—GETTY IMAGES

'My court is not a jester court ... I understand that people are starstruck. I'm not one of them.'

BECKY DEAN-WALKER, a Texas judge, after a county prosecutor said he'd recommend that musician Willie Nelson, who was facing charges of marijuana possession from November 2010, sing in court as part of a plea deal

'These people did not go away. They just went from hopey to mopey.'

VAN JONES, former Obama Administration official, discussing the young people who overwhelmingly supported Obama in the 2008 presidential race

'It's deeply bizarre and deeply creepy.'

VICTORIA NULAND, State Department spokeswoman, after an album of photos of former U.S. Secretary of State Condoleezza Rice was found in Muammar Gaddafi's Tripoli compound

'There are no secrets at our house. We tell the kids, "Mom and Dad are going off to kiss."'

BRAD PITT, in an interview with *USA Today,* on how he and Angelina Jolie make time for themselves while caring for their six children. The actor said when he and Jolie announce plans to sneak away, his kids reply, "Ewww, gross!"

'Bert and Ernie ... remain puppets and do not have a sexual orientation.'

SESAME WORKSHOP, in a statement responding to an online petition asking *Sesame Street* producers to let the longtime friends wed

'She even wanted to be late for her own funeral.'

SALLY MORRISON, Elizabeth Taylor's publicist, announcing that the Hollywood star's March 24 funeral began 15 minutes late, according to her final wishes

'I love that smell of the emissions.'

SARAH PALIN, *Tea Party icon, at a motorcycle rally in Washington*

TOP ROW, LEFT TO RIGHT: LARRY PAPKE—AP IMAGES; ALEX FRADKIN—REDUX. SECOND ROW: JASON MERRITT—GETTY IMAGES; STEVE GRANITZ—WIRE-IMAGE VIA GETTY IMAGES. THIRD ROW: PBS—COURTESY EVERETT COLLECTION; JOHN SPRINGER COLLECTION—CORBIS. BOTTOM: MANUEL BALCE CENETA—AP IMAGES

People of the Year

BIG SHOES TO FILL OF THE YEAR

In the Spotlight: Apple's New Leader

With the untimely passing of Steve Jobs on Oct. 5, former COO Tim Cook took over as the leader of computer giant Apple. So ... who is he? Cook, 51, grew up in Alabama, majored in industrial engineering at Auburn University and received an M.B.A. from Duke University's Fuqua School of Business in 1988. He spent 12 years at IBM before being hired by Compaq as a vice president in 1997. Six months later, he joined Apple, hired personally by Jobs to streamline the company's jumbled manufacturing and distribution operations.

Cook became Apple COO in 2007 and ran the company during Jobs' medical leaves. On one subject, he has strong opinions: when asked by FORTUNE magazine in 2008 if he could foresee replacing Jobs, Cook replied, "No, he's irreplaceable."

BROADCAST MOVERS OF THE YEAR

Do Touch That Dial

It was a year when TV's talking heads indulged their wanderlust (or ratings lust). A host of hosts sought new pastures, and the fat lady sang for a long-running soap opera.

Anderson Cooper

He already travels extensively for his CNN prime-time show, *Anderson Cooper 360°*, but the TV journalist, 44, took a detour in 2011, when he launched a syndicated daytime talk show, *Anderson*, in September.

Katie Couric

When her decision to leave NBC's *Today* show for the anchor chair at the *CBS Evening News* hadn't paid off after five years, Couric, 54, weighed her offers and joined ABC News; her daytime talk show will debut in 2012.

Oprah Winfrey

Her 25-year run as queen of daytime talk shows ended with a bang on May 25; Winfrey, 57, departed to lead her own cable channel. "I'm about as calm as a person who's about to give birth to such a humongous baby can be," Oprah opined.

Susan Lucci

Say it ain't so, ABC! When the network said on April 14 that it would cancel *All My Children*, 41 years of memories (and 11 wedding ceremonies for Erica Kane) went up in smoke. At least Lucci, 64, won an Emmy in 1999, after 19 nominations.

TIME-WASTER OF THE YEAR

Today's Rage, Tomorrow's Trivia Question

The new digital world we inhabit is a never-ending cornucopia of utterly unpredictable fads. Case in point: Angry Birds, the 2009 creation of obscure Finnish firm Rovio Mobile, in which players hurl grumpy fowl at a castle. Total downloads since launch: 350 million. Estimated total sales in 2011: $73-143 million. Now we know how an angry bird sounds: *Ka-ching!*

COOK: KEVORK DJANSEZIAN—GETTY IMAGES; TV, FROM TOP: ANDREW H. WALKER—GETTY IMAGES; HEATHER WINES—CBS VIA GETTY IMAGES; CHARLES REX ARBOGAST—AP IMAGES; EUGENE GOLOGURSKY—WIREIMAGE—GETTY IMAGES. BIRDS: NO CREDIT

OVEREXPOSED TV HOST OF THE YEAR

Grace Under Pressure

Georgia-born Nancy Grace, 52, is a former prosecutor who enjoys the limelight, as she proved when she appeared on ABC's glittery twirlfest, *Dancing with the Stars.* But when it came to the trial of Casey Anthony, the young Florida mother accused of killing daughter Caylee, 2, Grace didn't dance around the issues: in her one-sided analysis on her HLN cable-TV talk show, Anthony, a.k.a. "Tot Mom," was guilty, guilty, guilty—and retribution was due. Case closed!

Millions of viewers agreed with the woman TIME media critic James Poniewozik dubbed a "tabloid Torquemada." But 12 people with a closer view of the case—Anthony's jury—did not.

FUGITIVE OF THE YEAR

Bulger: Nabbed

Boston's infamous Irish mob boss James ("Whitey") Bulger boasted many alleged crimes: extortion, money laundering, drug dealing and at least 18 murders. He was No. 2 on the FBI's most-wanted list, but after 16 years on the lam, his trail seemed cold.

Or not: Bulger, 82, and longtime companion Catherine Greig were arrested on June 22 at an apartment house in Santa Monica, Calif., where they were living under assumed identities.

SCANDALS OF THE YEAR

Falling from the Heights

Arnold Schwarzenegger

"While I deserve your attention and criticism, my family does not," said the former California governor and Hollywood's Terminator, 64. On May 17 Arnold Schwarzenegger admitted that he had fathered a child, now 14 years old, with a member of his household staff. Wife Maria Shriver left their home before the celebrity couple announced their separation on May 9, after 25 years of marriage.

Shriver, 55, filed for divorce on July 1. The couple has four children. On July 17, their son Christopher, 13, was seriously injured in a surfing accident at Malibu Beach, but he is expected to make a full recovery.

Anthony Weiner

Representative Anthony Weiner of New York City ruined his career when he not only tweeted lewd photos of himself to a 21-year-old college student but also lied about it. "I lied because I was embarrassed," the seven-term Congressman admitted at a June 6 press conference. "I have made terrible mistakes." Under increasing fire, the Democrat, who had been considered as a potential successor to Mayor Michael Bloomberg, stepped down June 16.

Weiner, 47, fueled the frenzy, at first describing the tweets as a hack and a prank, before he eventually came clean and apologized to both his wife and the public.

MELTDOWN OF THE YEAR

Act Out, Lash Out, Flame Out

His high-octane, erratic lifestyle used to work for bad-boy actor Charlie Sheen, 46, star of the hit CBS sitcom *Two and a Half Men.* But in 2011 the star went off the rails. In February, Sheen, perhaps on a bender, granted interviews in which he insulted colleagues on the show and bragged about his offstage, R-rated sex-and-drug antics. Sheen next launched a nationwide speaking tour that ended early, amid chaos; before long, he was fired from the sitcom. Ashton Kutcher replaced him in May.

Sheen denied being influenced by drugs or alcohol, but his family, including his father, actor Martin Sheen, said he was indeed battling addiction. And while there's nothing humorous about addiction, Sheen's unfiltered quotes earned a place in the annals of swagger. A sampler:

- *"I'm on a drug. It's called Charlie Sheen. It's not available. If you try it once, you will die."*
- *"I'm tired of pretending like I'm not special. I'm tired of pretending like I'm not bitchin', a total freaking rock star from Mars."*

GRACE: ADAM TAYLOR—ABC; BULGER: U.S. MARSHALS SERVICE VIA AP IMAGES; SCHWARZENEGGER: STEVE YEATER—AP IMAGES; WEINER: MARIO TAMA—GETTY IMAGES; SHEEN: TOM BRIGLIA—GETTY IMAGES

Nation

Memorial service at New York City's World Trade Center on Sept. 11, 2011

DAVID HANDSCHUH—POOL—GETTY IMAGES

On the move *On Nov. 17, Occupy Wall Street marchers in Manhattan protest their eviction from Zuccotti Park*

DON EMMART—AFP—GETTY IMAGES

NATION

Challenging the Empire of Wealth

Occupy Wall Street protesters focus new attention on the inequities of the world's economies

THE MOVEMENT STARTED IN CANADA, OF ALL places, where the editors of the Vancouver-based anticonsumerist magazine *Adbusters* called for a "Tahrir Square moment" on Sept. 17 in lower Manhattan to protest what they called the disproportionate power of the U.S. corporate élite. The first responders, a motley collection of punks, anarchists, socialists, hackers, liberals and artists, spent that night in Zuccotti Park, an acre of concrete and greenery near Ground Zero, the New York Stock Exchange and the New York Federal Reserve. Then they did it again. Soon, others joined in: the unemployed and the underemployed, scenesters and community organizers, middle-aged activists and folks who don't bother to vote. The crowds swelled, both online and beneath New York's skyscrapers. Camera crews arrived. Celebrities made pilgrimages, and the spark started a fire.

They called themselves the Occupy Wall Street movement, and Facebook sign-up data suggested their num-

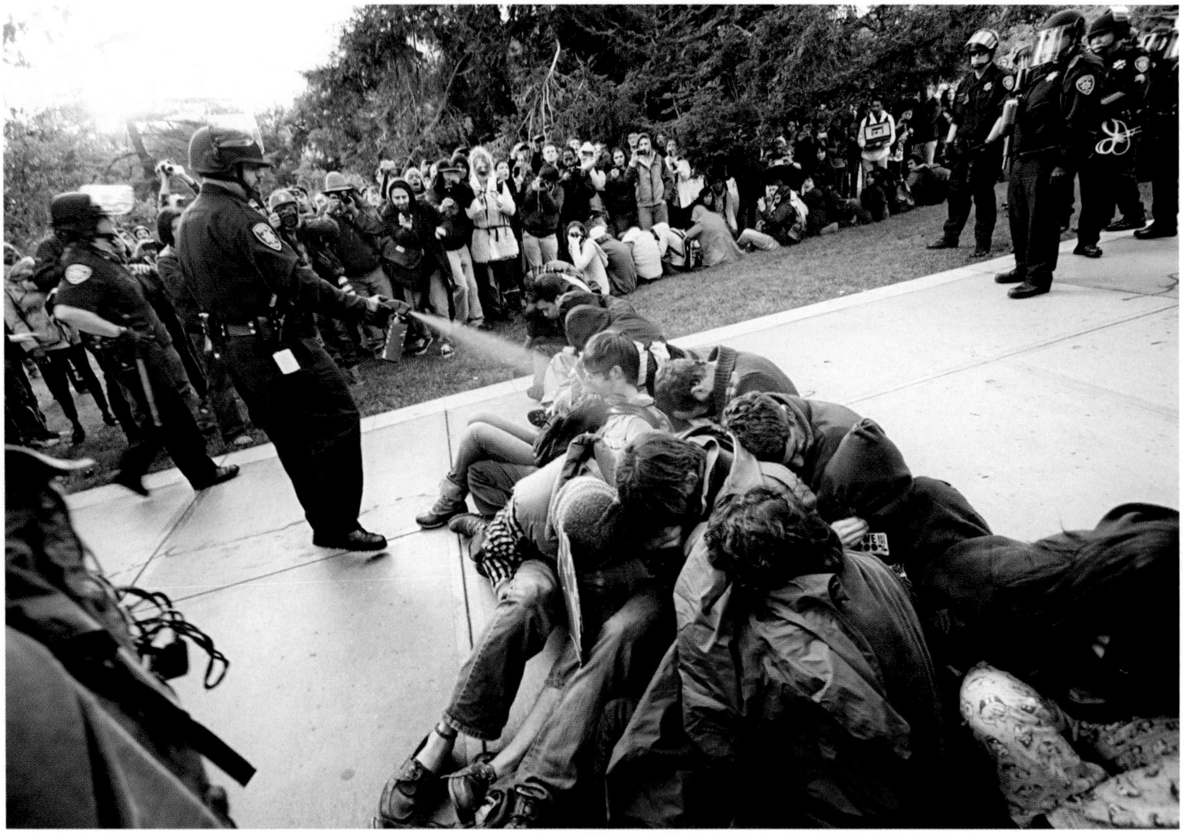

Uncalled for? *A University of California, Davis, police officer sprays pepper gas on passive students on Nov. 18*

bers were doubling in size, on average, every three days since mid-September. On Oct. 1, protesters marched from Wall Street to the Brooklyn Bridge, where they stopped traffic and confronted police, who arrested 700 of the Occupiers. The march and arrests did their job, generating a worldwide flurry of publicity for the movement. By Oct. 10, protesters in almost every state had joined the movement, and demonstrations had jumped the Pacific to Hong Kong, Tokyo and Sydney. Crowds gathered in Los Angeles, Albuquerque, Toledo, Knoxville and Fairbanks. Their growing numbers raised urgent questions: Who are these people, and what do they want?

The answers were as varied as the crowds, but a few threads emerged: embracing the motto "We Are the 99%," the U.S. protesters claimed to represent the vast majority of Americans, who have been languishing economically while the wealthiest 1% flourish. Corporations and banks, protesters said, have too much influence in Washington. Justin Ruben, executive director of MoveOn.org, which supported the Occupy effort, declared, "Inequality is suddenly a topic of conversation in politics." Many protesters urged higher taxes on the well-to-do and corporations; others talked of launching a consumer boycott of the big banks in favor of credit unions.

There was a New Deal–era charm to the encampment in Zuccotti Park, where a "People's Library" with 5,000 volumes was established. The protesters' daily schedule included smaller marches during the stock market's opening and closing bells and twice-daily meetings called general assemblies. A favorite tactic was the use of "human microphones," in which a speaker would say a few words, then pause while they were chanted by the crowd.

As the enthusiasm for the Occupy movement rose, the protests spread overseas. In London some 2,000 people gathered on Oct. 15 on the steps of St. Paul's Cathedral, where they greeted the ultimate rebel, WikiLeaks founder Julian Assange, as a hero. Though the crowd was substantial, it did not achieve its goal of Occupying the London Stock Exchange, where marchers found police barricades waiting. As an alternative, the crowd settled for returning to the nearby St. Paul's. The next morning the church's canon chancellor, the Rev. Giles Fraser, asked the police to leave the cathedral steps, insisting that the Occupy demonstrators had a right to protest peacefully. But as the encampment at the cathedral grew, protesters ignored the church's requests that they depart; ultimately, it was Fraser who stepped down.

WAYNE TILCOCK—THE ENTERPRISE—AP IMAGES

Ticked off *At top left, campers occupy New York City's Zuccotti Park. At top right, a Manhattan businessman squares off with a demonstrator. At bottom left, Occupiers gather in Frankfurt, Germany, near the euro symbol in front of the European Central Bank. At bottom right, police arrest a marcher in New York City on Nov. 17*

In Rome a major protest on Oct. 15th turned ugly and violent as a small minority of some 100,000 marchers confronted the police. By late afternoon, the protest had devolved into a full-scale battle, with police vans engaging in charges against hundreds of rock-throwing protesters. Tear gas floated like mist through the streets, as demonstrators barricaded the roads with metal barriers and trash bins. The violence robbed the march of its moral authority, as most of the protesters themselves voiced sympathy for the police and outrage at the minority who had tarnished the demonstration.

In the U.S., the Occupy movement's largest stronghold outside New York City was Oakland, Calif., where protesters showed their muscle on Nov. 2, calling for a general strike on a nationwide "Day of Mass Action." The day's protests shut down the bustling port, where as many as 7,000 people gathered peacefully to stop trucks in their tracks. But as in Rome, anarchists tried to hijack the proceedings in the final hours of the protest, and police used tear gas to subdue them.

Indeed, by mid-November the movement's charm had begun to wear thin, and with winter coming on across the country, authorities began to clamp down on the protesters. On Nov. 14, police cleared out the home base of the Occupy Oakland movement, across from city hall, meeting almost no resistance from the last protesters on the site. On Nov. 15 in Manhattan, hundreds of police officers, the majority clad in riot gear, encircled Zuccotti Park shortly after 1 a.m. Protesters were allowed to leave the space with some of their belongings, but they were warned that tarps and tents would no longer be permitted in the park. Many dug in and chained themselves around the Occupiers' central kitchen area in a forlorn last stand. About 70 protesters were arrested by police over the course of a three-hour operation, including some who chained themselves together. When dawn broke, the park had been cleaned and was no longer Occupied.

But if enthusiasm for the protests was waning in the cities, it was heating up on college campuses—and was given a boost by a ham-handed police clampdown on the campus of the University of California, Davis, on Friday, Nov.

The left was fighting back with its own iconography: fewer tricorn hats and more tattoos

CLOCKWISE FROM TOP LEFT: SPENCER PLATT—GETTY IMAGES; TODD MAISEL—NY DAILY NEWS VIA GETTY IMAGES; CHANG W. LEE—THE NEW YORK TIMES—REDUX; THOMAS LOHNES—AP IMAGES

18. A nonviolent protest turned chaotic that afternoon, as videos of the scene showed a policeman walking up to seated protesters, pulling out his can of pepper spray to display to the surrounding crowd, and liberally sweeping the protesters with the stinging substance. Other officers then followed suit, spraying many of the pasive Occupiers, as the watching crowd chanted "Shame on you!" The afternoon ended with 10 arrests, nine of them students.

By midday Saturday, videos of the showdown were circulating across the Internet, provoking cries of outrage around the nation. UC Davis chancellor Linda Katehi placed campus police chief Annette Spicuzza and the two officers shown spraying the students on leave, but many voices called for Katehi herself to step down.

From early in the Occupy movement's run, it was clear that the larger public was listening to its message. An Oct. 9-10 TIME/Abt SRBI poll found that 54% of Americans had a favorable view of the protests, despite the images of bearded and shirtless youth playing bongo drums, rolling cigarettes and painting their bodies in Zuccotti Park. The same poll found just 27% still had a favorable view of the Tea Party.

The protest benefited in its incipient stages by venting a broad array of common frustrations, many of them so vague that even Republicans could co-sign them. In TIME's poll, 86% of those familiar with the protests agreed with the contention that Wall Street and its proxies in Washington exert too much influence over the political process. Nearly 80% of respondents (96% of Democrats and 56% of Republicans) thought the class chasm between rich and poor is too large, and 68%, including 40% of Republicans, said the affluent should pay more taxes. Yet by mid-November some Americans applauded presidential candidate Newt Gingrich when he advised protesters to "Go get a job right after you take a bath."

It is far too early to judge the legacy of the Occupy movement. But recent experience suggests that small and spontaneous protests can matter in times of broad economic difficulty, whether in Arab dictatorships or advanced democracies. In 2009 a few dozen conservative activists found one another on Twitter, and the Tea Party began to grow. It came to define the national political conversation in the U.S., helping deliver Republican control of the House in 2010. Now the left was fighting back with the same toolkit and its own iconography—fewer tricorn hats, more tattoos. In Washington, no one dared to underestimate the potential impact of the protests. The message from the streets indicated that the status quo in U.S. politics was changing, just as the nation was gearing up for a presidential election in 2012. ■

Uncle Sam's Economy: Stuck in the Doldrums

However deeply divided on politics, Americans could agree on one thing in 2011: the economy was busted. Unemployment was still high, the housing market was weak, and the long-awaited economic recovery had yet to materialize.

Unemployment **On Oct. 7, the U.S. Bureau of Labor Statistics announced that the nation's unemployment rate was 9.1%, and that some 14 million Americans were out of work. In contrast, from 1948 until 2010 the U.S. unemployment rate averaged 5.7%. The rate dropped to 8.6% in November, suggesting that 2012 might bring an uptick in jobs.**

Retail Sales **Though the closing of such familiar stores as the Borders bookstore chain grabbed the headlines, retail sales were one of the stronger aspects of the economy in 2011. They increased 1.1% in September, the biggest gain in seven months, with strong auto sales leading the rise.**

Housing Market **After improving slightly in 2010, the U.S. housing market slumped again in 2011. Home values posted the largest decline in the year's first quarter since late 2008, falling 3%. Mortgage rates were near their lowest levels in decades, but tough loan standards disqualified many would-be buyers. Result: a stagnant market in which sales lagged and new-home construction was stalled throughout the summer and fall.**

FROM TOP: JUSTIN SULLIVAN—GETTY IMAGES; IAN NICHOLSON—PA VIA GETTY IMAGES; JOHN RAOUX—AP IMAGES

Going nowhere *Speaker of the House Boehner and President Obama tried but failed to forge a "grand bargain" on the budget*

KRISTOFFER TRIPPLAAR—POOL—GETTY IMAGES

Potomac Gridlock

Battles between Congress and the White House send public approval of the government into free-fall

"THE WORLD ONCE LOOKED AT AMERICA WITH awe as we built the interstate highway system, created the best public education in the world, put a man on the moon and invested in the frontiers of knowledge," TIME's Fareed Zakaria wrote in the wake of the late-summer struggle between Congress and the White House over raising the nation's debt ceiling. "That is not how the world sees America today ... We have taken something that the world never doubted—the credibility of the U.S.—and put it into question."

In 2011, the partisan rancor that has gripped the capital since Republicans won control of the House of Representatives in the 2010 election reached new heights, until the government itself seemed paralyzed and unable to function. The crunch came on what has always been a relatively minor legislative act: the periodic need for Congress to approve a raising of the government's debt ceiling. But with Congress and the public focusing on the nation's troubled economy amid mounting fears over the size of the federal debt, Republicans seized on the vote as an opportunity to stop the fiscal bleeding they believed was at the heart of the economic slump. Rejecting attempts by President Barack Obama and Speaker of the House John Boehner that would have called for compromise on both sides, nicknamed a "grand bargain," Republicans achieved a victory on their terms, successfully resisting all attempts by Democrats to include tax increases as part of the plan. On July 31, Obama and Boehner announced that a deal had been struck in which the debt ceiling would be raised, but government spending would be sharply cut to allow for the increased debt.

Under the complex agreement, dubbed the Budget Control Act of 2011, $917 billion would be cut over 10 years in exchange for increasing the debt limit by $900 billion. A Congressional Joint Select Committee, consisting of six members from each party, would produce debt reduction legislation by Nov. 23, 2011, that would be immune from amendments or filibuster. The goal is to cut at least $1.5 trillion more in spending over the coming 10 years. If the committee fails to agree on the areas where the cuts would occur, it would trigger across-the-board cuts ("sequestration"), equally split between defense and non-defense programs. The legislation passed the House on Aug. 1, 2011, by a vote of 269 to 161. The Senate passed the agreement on Aug. 2 by a vote of 74 to 26.

The deal over what had previously been a minor matter dominated Washington from May through July—and it left many Americans furious with the leaders of both parties. Gallup polls showed that only 13% of Americans had a positive view of Congress in August, tying a historic low. President Obama's approval ratings also dropped to a new low, 40%, on July 29. Another victim of the brouhaha was the Tea Party, the right-wing GOP movement whose adherents pushed representatives not to compromise during the debate. In a late September CNN/ORC International poll, 53% of those polled held a negative view of the Tea Party, with just 28% supporting it.

"Ironically, during this period, more and more Americans identify as independents," Zakaria wrote. "Registered independents are at an all-time high. But that doesn't matter. The system in Congress reflects not rule by the majority but rule by the minority—fanatical, organized minorities ... In area after area—energy, immigration, infrastructure—government policy is suboptimal, a sad mixture of political payoffs and ideological positioning. Countries from Canada to Australia to Singapore implement smart policies and copy best practices from around the world. We bicker and remain paralyzed." ■

Scenes from a Fractured Nation

How to measure the nation's polarization? A *National Journal* study showed that, for the first time since the publication began tracking the political divide 30 years ago, the most left-wing Republican in Congress is more conservative than the most right-wing Democrat.

On the Left **A bitter battle over the budget in Wisconsin echoed the national divide, as GOP legislators passed a bill that balanced a $3.6 billion shortfall by, in part, limiting the collective bargaining rights of public employee unions. Democratic Senators fled the state to delay a vote, and unions launched massive protests in the capital, above, but the bill was successfully passed on March 10.**

On the Right **The Tea Party is a minority within the Grand Old Party, but its vocal, politically active members—shown above marching against the controversial deal to raise the nation's debt ceiling—wield a disproportionate influence within it. Speaking for many in the Tea Party, Representative Michele Bachmann said, "I will vote against any proposal that includes tax increases or raises the debt ceiling."**

LEFT: NICOLE BENGIVENO—THE NEW YORK TIMES—REDUX; WIN MCNAMEE—GETTY IMAGES

PROFILE

Eric Cantor

The House majority leader thwarted the White House agenda

PALE-FACED, BESPECTACLED AND INTENSE, House majority leader Eric Cantor can't seem to sit still and appears to subsist on a regimen of tuna sandwiches and diet soda. A Richmond, Va., native who likes to brag that he holds the seat once graced by James Madison, Cantor, 48, earned degrees from George Washington University, William & Mary and Columbia University. He met his wife, investment banker Diana Fine, on a blind date and went into his family's well-established financial-services business before being elected to the Virginia house of delegates in 1991. A decade later, in the first year of George W. Bush's presidency, he went to Congress, where he has enjoyed a meteoric rise. The highest ranking Jewish member of Congress in history, Cantor describes himself as "a minority within a minority," a Jew from the South, whose political views are often at odds with those of most urban Jewish voters.

After the Republicans took control of the lower house of Congress in 2010, Cantor helped lead the GOP Representatives in their year-long crusade to lower taxes and cut spending. As party leaders, he and Speaker of the House John Boehner match up well. Boehner has been the good cop to Cantor's firmer hand, and the two have kept the House Republicans united in vote after vote against President Barack Obama's proposals. There is a measure of rivalry in their relationship: Cantor did not back Boehner for the top party job and has made little secret of his own ambitions. Yet the majority leader played no small role in parrying Democrats at every turn and achieving major budget victories for conservatives in 2011, and it was Cantor whom Boehner tapped to lead negotiations with the White House at the height of the tense debt-ceiling negotiations in July.

Cantor has emerged as the Newt Gingrich of his generation, a wonky, partisan bomb thrower who is increasingly popular with Republicans around the country and has become a potent fund raiser for GOP candidates and causes. He did not pursue the presidential nomination in 2012, but he is known to be a man who takes a long view of life—and politics. ■

TOM WILLIAMS—ROLL CALL—GETTY IMAGES

PROFILE

Paul Ryan

The Republicans' House policy pro offers a roadmap for the future

WISCONSIN REPRESENTATIVE PAUL RYAN, the Republican Party's baby-faced budget wonk, has for years proposed dramatic changes to federal spending and entitlement programs. But after GOP midterm victories in 2010 gave the party a House majority, Ryan's 75-page budget-balancing proposal went from mere Tea Party wish list to the central policy platform of the Republicans. The House passed Ryan's ambitious budget plan, *The Path to Prosperity,* thrusting the issue of deficit reduction into President Obama's lap and setting the stage for months of debate and discord. Democrats, in turn, seized on Ryan's entitlement proposals as an electoral issue, rallying around a defense of Medicare to win a key special congressional election in May.

Win some, lose some. But the conversation about red ink in Washington continues to be dictated in no small part by Ryan's vision, even though he does not always march in lockstep with his GOP colleagues: he defied party doctrine by supporting both the Troubled Asset Relief Program and the auto-industry bailout. The telegenic supply-side conservative cut his teeth as a speechwriter for Jack Kemp and Bill Bennett in the mid-1990s. After serving as legislative director for Kansas Senator Sam Brownback, Ryan mounted a successful bid for Wisconsin's First Congressional District seat in 1998, at age 28. Now 40, the avid outdoorsman is ensconced in a district that shares his pro-life, pro-gun views, and has ascended to become the ranking Republican on the House Budget Committee.

Ryan's budget plan was called "courageous" by many pundits but was savaged by Democrats as simply one more plan to protect the rich at the expense of the poor. Ryan's reply: "I do believe government has a role in making sure we have a safety net to help people who cannot help themselves or are temporarily down on their luck. But I don't want to see government turn that safety net into a hammock." ■

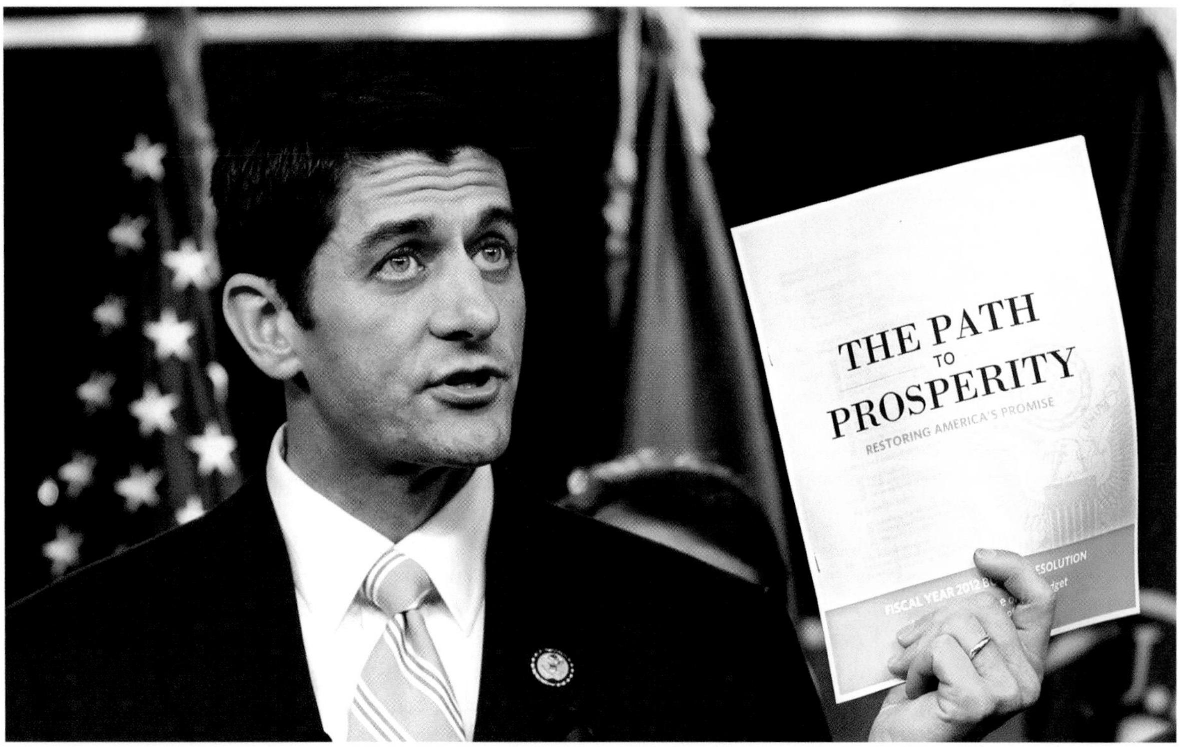

J. SCOTT APPLEWHITE—AP IMAGES

RICK SANTORUM, 53
Former U.S. Senator, Penn.
EARLY LINE: Known for his strong stands against abortion and homosexuality, he appealed to GOP "values voters"—but the year's focus was on the economy

NEWT GINGRICH, 68
Former Speaker of the House
EARLY LINE: Verbose, smart and at times pompous, Gingrich was hurt early on when his entire senior staff resigned in June, but he was riding high in the polls by December

MICHELE BACHMANN, 55
U.S. Representative, Minn.
EARLY LINE: A favorite of the Christian right, Bachmann was seen as a charismatic, Palin-like figure early on, yet she lost some traction when Perry entered the race

MITT ROMNEY, 64
Former governor, Mass.
EARLY LINE: The front runner as the race began, Romney was judged the best performer in early debates. Even so, by December Gingrich was pressing him hard

RICK PERRY, 61
Governor of Texas
EARLY LINE: Well funded and very popular at home, Perry jumped into the contest late and found fans quickly. Yet a weak showing in the early debates set back his cause

And They're Off! GOP candidates vie to challenge President Obama

Save the picture above as a keepsake: these are the eight Republican candidates who remained in the race to face President Barack Obama in the 2012 election, as of the party's fifth debate, held Sept. 7 in California, after one other candidate, Tim Pawlenty, dropped out and several other popular figures decided not to run. With Obama's approval ratings sliding downhill throughout the year, there was a good chance that one of them might be occupying the Oval Office as of Jan. 20, 2013.

From early in the race, second-time candidate Mitt Romney was the front runner, thanks to his familiarity, presidential bearing, command of the issues and business experience. But Romney's Mormon religion, the controversial health plan he installed as governor of Massachusetts and his centrist views were anathema to the party's base voters, who exert outsized influence in the GOP primary contests. These outspoken voices strongly favored a Tea Party–friendly, red-meat conser-

RICH SCHMITT—ZUMA PRESS—CORBIS

RON PAUL, 76
U.S. Representative, Texas
EARLY LINE: The libertarian 12-term Congressman is a hero to many voters on the right. Still, he struggled to translate his intellectual appeal into funds and support

HERMAN CAIN, 66
Former CEO, Godfather's Pizza
EARLY LINE: Cain found early support with an innovative proposal for a U.S. tax over-haul. But charges of sexual harassment and a long-term affair led to his withdrawal

JON HUNTSMAN, 51
Former governor, Utah
EARLY LINE: Obama's accomplished and thoughtful former ambassador to China was widely respected. Even so, he battled to attract funding, media coverage and fans early in the race

vative rather than Romney, a Massachusetts moderate.

Several candidates were anointed as the anti-Romney, but most stumbled. Michele Bachmann's appeal faded when Rick Perry entered the race; then Perry faltered in a series of debates, unable in one even to recall his anti-Washington talking points. Herman Cain rode a boomlet but withdrew, hurt by charges of sexual misconduct during his days as a restaurant industry lobbyist and by his inability to recall his stance on Libya in an interview with the Milwaukee *Journal Sentinel* editorial board.

As of early December, former House Speaker Newt Gingrich—whose campaign had seemed dead in the water only months before—had become the strongest alternative to Romney and was rising steadily in the polls, with 11 months to go before the general election. ■

On the Sidelines

With the GOP race in a highly fluid state throughout the year, one candidate withdrew early, while others tested the water to measure support, only to decide against seeking the nomination.

Chris Christie New Jersey's governor, 49, enjoys a wide following, thanks to his caustic, witty comments on politics and society. When Rick Perry stumbled in early debates, calls for Christie to run surged, and he considered doing so. But on Oct. 4, he disappointed supporters when he declared, "Now is not my time," and within days, he endorsed front runner Romney.

Mitch Daniels The governor of Indiana, 62, is a former Bush Administration budget office director who is widely regarded as smart, moderate and effective. Many Republicans urged him to run as a centrist against the right-wing pack, but though Daniels placed high in some early straw polls, he declared on May 22 that he would not seek the presidency.

Sarah Palin The party's charismatic 2008 V.P. candidate, 47, commands the affections of a large segment of the Republican base. Her bus tours, motorcycle rides and speeches throughout the year kept alive the possibility that she might join the race. But on Oct. 5 she declared she would not make the run, deeply disappointing her admirers.

Tim Pawlenty The well-regarded former governor of Minnesota, 51, signalled early on that he might run, and he announced his candidacy on May 23. Though in other years he might have appeared a strong conservative, he found little favor with the Tea Party, and on Aug. 14 he became the first candidate to withdraw, later throwing his support to Romney.

FROM TOP: JEFF ZELEVANSKY—GETTY IMAGES; TOM WILLIAMS—ROLL CALL—GETTY IMAGES; JUSTIN SULLIVAN—GETTY IMAGES; SPENCER PLATT—GETTY IMAGES

A Tragedy In Tucson

A deranged gunman opens fire as a Congresswoman meets with constituents, leaving six people dead

THE DATE: JAN. 8, 2011. THE PLACE: THE PARKING lot of La Toscana Village, a strip shopping center in the northern hills of Tucson, Ariz., where Representative Gabrielle (Gabby) Giffords was due to host a meet-and-greet with her constituents. "My 1st Congress on Your Corner starts now," the third-term Democrat tweeted from her iPad just before 10 a.m. "Please stop by to let me know what is on your mind."

Giffords, 41, was a Democrat in a Republican-leaning district that is struggling with the divisive issues of immigration and border security. So the meeting wouldn't be a lovefest. Some of those peaceably assembling were there to tell Giffords how much they admired her, and some intended to give her a piece of their mind. But such exchanges never happened, not after Jared Loughner, 22, wearing a hoodie and sunglasses, arrived on the scene in a taxicab. After getting change from a Safeway cashier to pay the cabdriver, he then walked up to Representative Giffords and leveled a Glock 19 pistol at her head.

Loughner was a desperately confused young man whose grasp on reality had slipped. After the fact, psychiatrist E. Fuller Torrey, reviewing the symptoms and trajectory of Loughner's behavior in recent years, declared, "Chances are 99% that

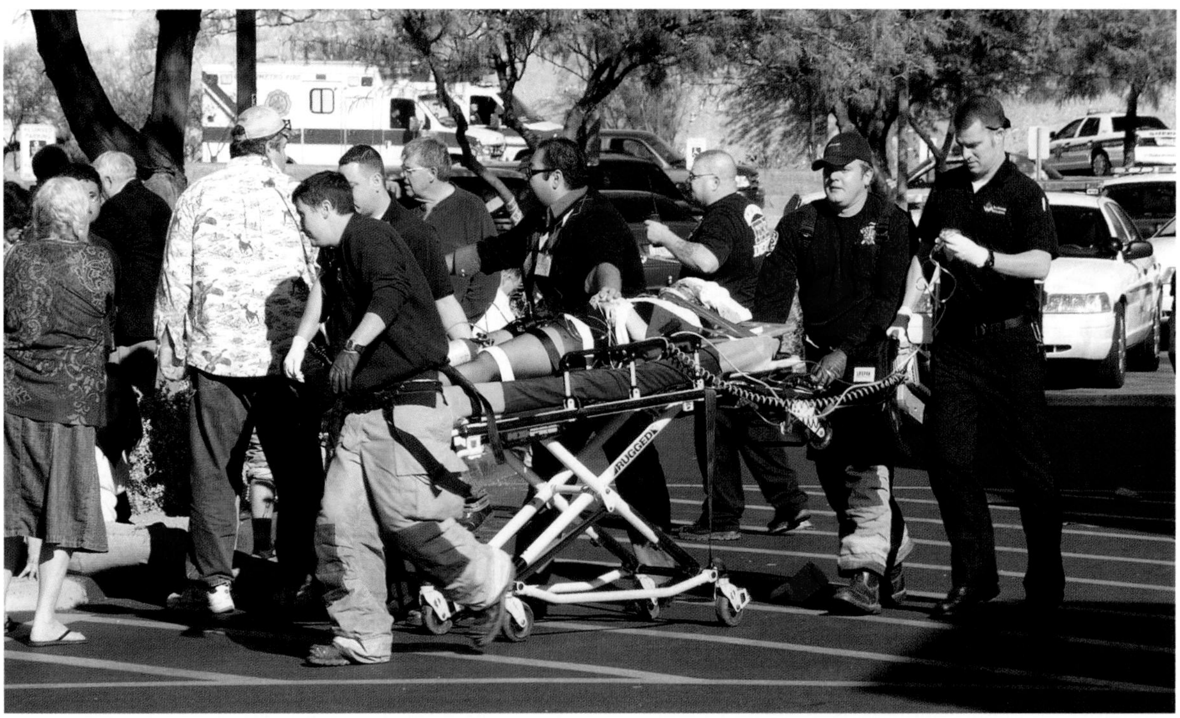

JAMES F. PALKA—ZUMAPRESS.COM

Gunned down *After a bullet fired at close range passed through her head, Giffords is rushed to a hospital*

he has schizophrenia." Loughner's tale is familiar: he was a nice, friendly boy until his mid-teens, when things began to go awry. He began drinking heavily and doing drugs. By age 20, he had begun to entertain bizarre belief systems; at times he claimed that he was a victim of government mind control.

In the fall of 2010 Loughner was attending Pima Community College, hoping to get his life on track. But his strange outbursts and unsettling demeanor spooked fellow students, who complained. Five weeks into the term, the college suspended Loughner, telling him that he could not return until he had a letter from a mental-health professional certifying that he was not dangerous. He didn't return. But he did buy a gun.

The first bullet he fired struck Giffords in the head, tunneled through the left side of her brain and exited. As she slumped to the pavement, Loughner sprayed 30 additional rounds into the crowd, wounding 18 more people, six of them mortally. Horrified onlookers quickly responded: one man grabbed a folding chair and smashed it across Loughner's back. As the gunman staggered, his left arm extended, and Bill Badger, a retired U.S. Army colonel, grabbed it and shoved him to the ground. Others joined in, until the killer was finally subdued.

Loughner

A federal grand jury quickly indicted Loughner on 49 counts, including the attempted assassination of a U.S. Congresswoman and several murder charges, but he may never stand trial. On May 25, 2011, Federal Judge Larry Burns ruled Loughner incompetent to stand trial for mental reasons. As of late October 2011, he was being held in a federal hospital while prosecutors, judges and psychiatrists pondered his future.

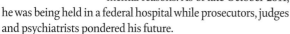

Against the odds, Gabby Giffords survived. Americans marveled as doctors told of the gradual return of her mental, vocal and motor skills. And they cheered when her husband, U.S. Navy Captain and astronaut Mark Kelly, undertook his scheduled flight aboard the space shuttle *Endeavour* in May.

On Aug. 1, a recovering Giffords, unsteady but smiling, received a standing ovation on the floor of the House of Representatives when she returned to cast a vote in favor of the controversial agreement to raise the U.S. federal debt ceiling. Her appearance marked a happy moment at the end of a bitter debate. Another debate—whether tragedies like the one in Tucson can ever be stopped—deserves to continue. ■

"My 1st Congress on Your Corner starts now. Please stop by to let me know what's on your mind."

—GIFFORDS TWEET, JUST BEFORE THE SHOOTINGS

Homecoming *Giffords returns to the floor of the House, accompanied by husband Mark Kelly, a NASA astronaut*

The Gunman's Victims

Ordinary people caught up in an extraordinary situation, they lost their lives. The courageous actions of their neighbors stopped Loughner's shooting spree and spared further deaths

Christina Green **Just 9 years old—she was born on 9/11—Green was a newly elected member of her school's student council and was taking an interest in politics. She played second base in Little League and loved music, dance and swimming.**

Dorothy Morris **"Dot" Morris, 76, moved to Arizona from Reno, Nev., with her high school sweetheart. They were married for 55 years.**

John Roll **The 63-year-old jurist was the center of his community. Appointed by President George H.W. Bush, he had served as chief judge of the U.S. District Court of Arizona since 2006.**

Phyllis Schneck **The 79-year-old great-grandmother retired to Arizona from New Jersey. A lifelong Republican, she wanted to say a few admiring words to her Democratic Representative.**

Dorwan Stoddard **When the shooting started, the 76-year-old former construction worker, a daily volunteer at his church, shielded his wife from the spray of bullets. She survived; he did not.**

Gabe Zimmerman **Giffords' director of outreach since 2007, he was a social worker and an avid runner. The 30-year-old loved history and travel and was engaged to be married.**

TOP: TOM WILLIAMS—ROLL CALL—GETTY IMAGES; BOTTOM: PIMA COUNTY SHERIFF'S FORENSIC UNIT VIA GETTY IMAGES

DIANA WALKER—CONTOUR BY GETTY IMAGES

PROFILE

Hillary Rodham Clinton

The Secretary of State derives maximum benefit from limited power

A MAJOR VICTORY FOR U.S. FOREIGN POLICY didn't look much like a rousing red-white-and-blue win when seen at street level in Libya. Secretary of State Hillary Clinton disembarked from her C-17 Globemaster III in Tripoli on Oct. 18 and was greeted by a ragtag honor guard of victorious rebels in mismatched uniforms who then trailed her through empty, trash-strewn streets, swerving in and out of her motorcade, pointing their AK-47s into the air. Even the conflict's finale, which came two days later with the bloody, lawless shooting of the fallen dictator Muammar Gaddafi, suggested that vengeful chaos may rule, at least for a while, in Libya.

But this may just be what an American victory looks like in the 21st century: not brass bands and treaties on parchment but unruly insurgents and a promise (fingers crossed) to hold elections. It's fitting that the U.S.-led intervention yielded an uncertain result; from

On the fly *Clinton works a cell phone aboard a U.S. C-17, on her way to meet with rebel leaders in Tripoli*

"We can't wave a magic wand and say to China or Brazil or India, 'Quit growing' "

the start, the mission was as much about the limits of U.S. power as its expanse. To build support for allied attacks on Gaddafi's troops in March 2011, Clinton had to get Arab leaders behind the plan, lobby the Russians to sign on, convince Congress that other countries would bear most of the cost and placate the Pentagon by arranging for a quick hand-over of military command to NATO.

The Libyan war was a microcosm of Clinton's broader challenge: creating a 21st century statecraft for a world where social media and cell phones have empowered people relative to their rulers, a world where U.S. influence is limited not only by the rise of loose networks like al-Qaeda and fast-rising states like China but also by America's economic challenges and the public's lack of interest in foreign adventures.

Yet this new era offers the U.S. opportunities as well as obstacles. Through a smart combination of its still dominant military hard power and its subtler soft power in economics and technology, the U.S. is remaking its influence in the 21st century. "All power has limits," Clinton told TIME. "In a much more networked and multipolar world," she said, "we can't wave a magic wand and say to China or Brazil or India, 'Quit growing. Quit using your economies to assert power' ... It's up to us to figure out how we position ourselves to be as effective as possible."

Clinton is something of an expert in coming up with creative ways to maximize limited power. She has succeeded in her public career thanks to her unorthodox approach to the office of the First Lady and despite the constraints imposed by a White House run by her former political rival Barack Obama. Clinton, who turned 64 on Oct. 26, says she intends to leave her post after one term. But the public still finds her both fascinating—and a potential Commander in Chief. A TIME poll in early October found that Clinton does far better than Obama against potential 2012 GOP opponents, leading to speculation that she might run for President in 2016, something her closest staff dismiss.

For the moment, Clinton is pushing her agenda with a combination of record-setting travel (including a breakthrough visit to Burma in late November), new partnerships with private organizations and an effort to immerse all State Department personnel in social media, from entry-level foreign service officers to new ambassadors. "As we look at how we manage the Arab Spring," Clinton told TIME, "we are trying to influence the direction, with full recognition that we don't have ownership and we don't have control. And there's a lot that's going to happen that is unpredictable. But we want to lead by our values and our interests in ways that, regardless of the trajectory over the next decade, people will know the United States was on the side of democracy, on the side of the rule of law ... And that will, I hope, be a strong antidote to the voices of either fatalism or extremism." That is not exactly a realist's view of the changing 21st century world, or an idealist's. But Hillary Clinton is betting her legacy that it is a powerfully American one. ■

—By Massimo Calabresi

Over There. The U.S. military winds down its presence abroad

When Barack Obama was elected President in 2008, he was swept into office in part based upon his longtime opposition to the U.S. intervention in Iraq, begun in 2003 by President George W. Bush. Yet in one of the key decisions of his presidency, Obama increased the U.S. presence in Afghanistan, which had dwindled since the successful U.S.-led war that brought down the Taliban government late in 2001. On Dec. 1, 2009, Obama ordered 30,000 more U.S. troops to Afghanistan.

But by 2011, with the global and U.S. economies stuck in neutral, foreign affairs were no longer Job One for the President, and polls showed that Americans' focus had strongly turned to pocketbook issues. The challenge for the Obama Administration was to manage the endgames in both Iraq and Afghanistan, in hopes of removing as many U.S. troops as possible while leaving behind governments capable of defending themselves.

That task seemed far more achievable in Iraq than in Afghanistan. The Administration said it was on course to meet its goal of removing almost all U.S. troops from Iraq by year's end. In Afghanistan the situation was more fraught, with trust in two critical U.S. allies—the nation of neighboring Pakistan and the Afghan government led by Hamid Karzai—continuing to erode. The President was hewing to his timetable of removing 10,000 U.S. troops by Jan. 1, 2012, and all troops by 2014, but few observers believed that Afghanistan's internal problems would be solved if and when the last Yanks departed.

Al-Awlaki: Dispatched

In 2011 the U.S. ramped up its reliance on drone aircraft to fight terrorist groups around the world. Remote-controlled drones were used heavily in Afghanistan, Pakistan and Libya, and were deployed for the first time in Yemen. On Sept. 30, the program scored a major success when an unmanned craft launched a missile that killed charismatic U.S.-born terrorist kingpin Anwar al-Awlaki, 40, the leader of al-Qaeda in the Arabian Peninsula, who was involved in at least two foiled plots to explode bombs on U.S. soil.

Iraq: An Orderly Withdrawal

Memories are short in our fast-forward world, so it's hard to recall that as recently as 2006 there was a chorus of calls for the U.S. to pull out of Iraq because American efforts there seemed doomed. That was before Army General David Petraeus led the "surge" of 30,000 troops into Iraq that—with the essential assistance of the so-called Sunni awakening—led to a restive calm across the country. Violence in Iraq perked up late in the summer of 2011, but an agreement between Washington and Prime Minister Nouri al-Maliki still called for all U.S. troops to be out of Iraq by the end of 2011. As of mid-September, 45,000 troops remained, but the drawdown had begun, and the Pentagon said it was on track to meet the Dec. 31 deadline. Above, soldiers of Montana's 163rd Alpha Company prepare to head home.

As the new year approached, U.S. and Iraqi leaders were weighing whether some U.S. troops should remain into 2012, as Baghdad continued to struggle with internal instability and the burgeoning influence exercised by neighboring Iran. At one point, U.S. officials indicated they might be willing to keep some U.S. troops in Iraq past the deadline, but the plan was later dropped. There was also an asterisk in the process: while most U.S. soldiers will come home by Dec. 31, the Pentagon expects to keep several thousand private contractors—21st century camp followers—in Iraq.

Afghanistan: Still Unstable

In 2011, Operation Enduring Freedom officially became the longest war in U.S. history. But to see how far the U.S., its NATO allies and the embattled government of ally Hamid Karzai remain from victory, consider the events that took place early in the fall. On Sept. 13, a series of Taliban attacks rocked the capital, Kabul, for 20 hours as grenades landed inside the heavily fortified U.S. embassy. A week later, the group used a bomb hidden in an insurgent's turban to assassinate former Afghan President Burhanuddin Rabbani. In both cases, U.S. commanders said the Taliban received crucial support from the Pakistan-based Haqqani Network, an anti-U.S. group that is charged with being affiliated with Pakistan's ISI security agency. On Oct. 5, the former commander of U.S. troops in Afghanistan, General Stanley McChrystal, told the Council on Foreign Relations that after 10 years of fighting, the U.S. and NATO allies remain far from reaching their goals.

Far along or not, President Obama announced on June 22 that 10,000 U.S. troops would be withdrawn by the end of 2011, and that an additional 23,000 would depart by the summer of 2012. Those drawdowns would leave more than 65,000 U.S. troops—like those at left, on patrol in Helmand Province in January—in Afghanistan.

National Security: A Change at the Top

President Obama's national security team underwent a major shake-up in 2011, triggered by the retirement of Secretary of Defense Robert Gates, 68, on Jume 30. Gates, who also headed up the Pentagon under President George W. Bush, was widely respected for his evenhanded, collegial approach to his job. He had announced his departure well in advance.

Obama asked CIA Director Leon Panetta, 73, left—like Gates, a veteran Washington hand—to serve as Secretary of Defense; the military and the spy agency are working closely together as they battle terrorist threats around the world. The new coordination between the two was further underlined when Obama asked his commander in Afghanistan, General David Petraeus, 59, right, to take over from Panetta at the CIA. The changes were completed in September.

LEFT PAGE: MICHAEL KAMBER—POLARIS. RIGHT PAGE, TOP: SPENCER PLATT—GETTY IMAGES. MIDDLE: TRACEY WOODWARD—THE WASHINGTON POST VIA GETTY IMAGES. BOTTOM, FROM LEFT: BRENDAM SMIALOWSKI—GETTY IMAGES: SHAH MARAI—AFP—GETTY IMAGES

NATION

Justice, At Last

Mission accomplished: Osama bin Laden is found and killed

THE FOUR HELICOPTERS CHUFFED URGENTLY THROUGH the Khyber Pass, racing over the lights of Peshawar and down toward the quiet city of Abbottabad and the prosperous neighborhood of Bilal Town. In the dark houses below slept doctors, lawyers, retired military officers—and perhaps the world's most wanted fugitive. The U.S. birds were on their way to find out.

Ahead loomed a strange-looking house in a walled compound. The pilots knew it well, having trained for their mission using a specially built replica. The house was three stories tall, as if to guarantee a clear view of approaching threats, and the perimeter walls were higher and thicker than any ordinary resident would require. Another high wall shielded the upper balcony from view. A second, smaller house stood nearby. As a pair of backup helicopters orbited overhead, an HH-60 Pave Hawk chopper and a CH-47 Chinook dipped toward the compound. A dozen U.S. Navy SEALs fast-roped onto the roof of a building from the HH-60 before it lost its lift and landed hard against a wall. The Chinook landed, and its troops clambered out.

Half a world away, it was Sunday afternoon in the crowded White House Situation Room. President Barack Obama was stone-faced as he followed the unfolding drama on silent video screens—a drama he alone had the power to start but now was powerless to control. At a meeting three days earlier, Obama had heard his options summarized, three ways of dealing with tantalizing yet uncertain intelligence that had been developed over painstaking months and years. He could continue to watch the strange compound using spies and satellites in hopes that the prey would reveal himself. He could knock

WARWICK PAGE—THE NEW YORK TIMES—REDUX PICTURES

Terrorist's lair *Local gawkers gaze at the compound in Abbottabad, Pakistan, where al-Qaeda's leader was found and killed by U.S. troops*

Evidence *After U.S. troops blew up the helicopter that went down during the raid, local authorities cloaked its tail*

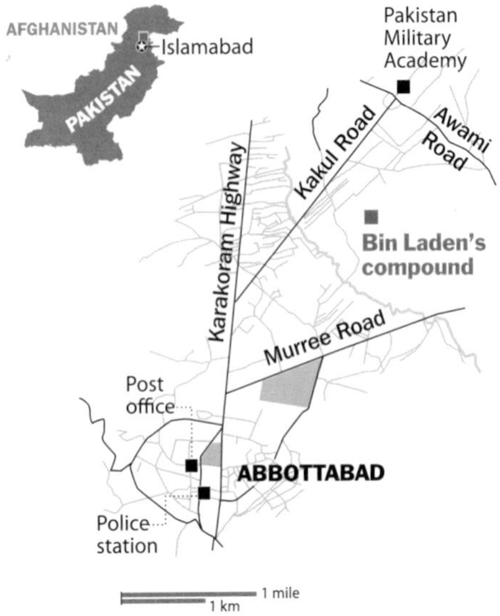

Bin Laden's Last Minutes
A decade in hiding comes to an end

1
A pair of helicopters carrying about 24 Seals **swoops in on the compound.** One chopperful fast-ropes in, while the other lands and disgorges its SEALs

out the building from a safe distance using B-2 bombers and their precision-guided payloads. Or he could unleash the special force of SEALs known as Team 6.

How strong was the intelligence? he asked. A 50% to 80% chance, he was told. What could go wrong? Plenty: a hostage situation, a diplomatic crisis—a dozen varieties of the sort of botch that ruins a presidency. To wait was to risk a leak, now that more than a hundred people had been briefed on the possible raid. To bomb might mean that the U.S. would never know for sure whether the mission was a success. As for an assault by special units, U.S. relations with the Pakistani government were tricky enough without staging a raid on sovereign territory.

Obama's inner circle was deeply divided. After more than an hour of discussion, he dismissed the group, saying he wanted time to reflect—but not much time. The next morning, as the President left the White House to tour tornado damage in Alabama, he paused on his way through the Diplomatic Reception Room to render his decision: Send the SEALs.

On Saturday the weather was cloudy in Abbottabad. Obama attended the White House Correspondents' Dinner, where a ballroom full of snoops had no inkling of the news volcano rumbling under their feet. The next morning, Obama joined his staff in the Situation Room as the mission lifted off from a base in Jalalabad, eastern Afghanistan. The bet was placed: U.S. choppers invaded the airspace of a foreign country without warning, to attack a walled compound housing unknown occupants.

As the birds swooped down on the mysterious house, the satellite feeds were addled for some 40 minutes. A hole was blown through the side of the house; gunfire erupted. Soms SEALs worked their way through the smaller buildings inside the compound. Others swarmed upward in the main building, floor by floor, until they came to the room where they hoped to find their cornered target. Then they were inside the room for a final burst of gunfire. What had happened? In Washington, the President sat and stared while several of his aides paced. The minutes "passed like days," one official recalls. The grounded chopper felt like a bad omen. Then a voice crackled with the hoped-for code name: "Visual on Geronimo."

Osama bin Laden, elusive leader of the al-Qaeda terrorist network, the man who said yes to the 9/11 attacks, the taunting voice and daunting catalyst of thousands of political murders on four continents, was dead. The U.S. had finally found the long-sought needle in a huge and dangerous haystack.

EPA

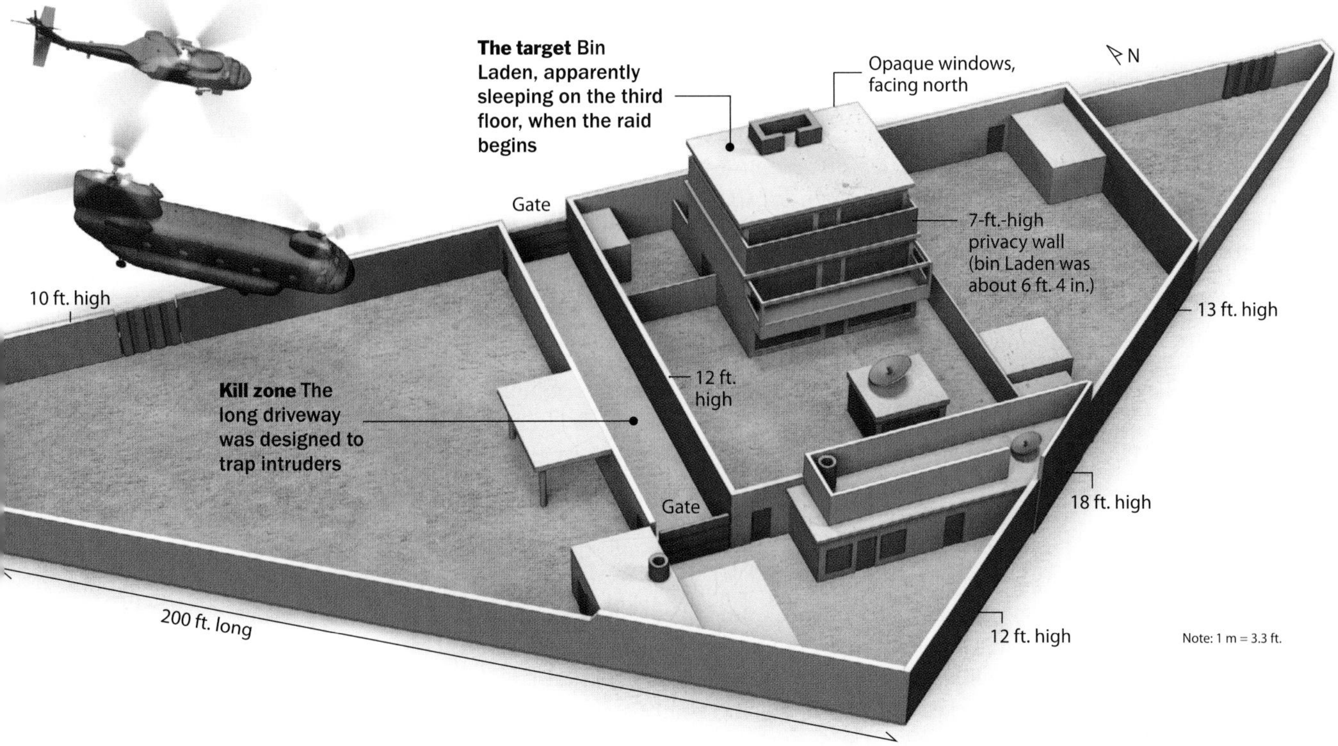

2 For most of the SEALs' 40 minutes on the ground, **the team engages in a firefight,** clearing the small building first, then reaching bin Laden and his family on the top two floors of the main building

3 In the final showdown, bin Laden is found with one of his wives in a bedroom. She is shot and wounded, and he is **killed by a shot over the left eye**

4 U.S. personnel sweep through the compound **collecting computers and documents** for later use by intelligence teams seeking information about al-Qaeda

5 One of the choppers, after landing with mechanical problems, **is destroyed** once remaining noncombatants have been moved safely away

6 The SEALs team **departs in the functioning chopper** and a backup, along with bin Laden's body

7 A coded message is sent to Washington—"Geronimo: E-KIA," indicating that **bin Laden is dead**

Source: U.S. Department of Defense

The path to Bin Laden began in the dark prisons of the CIA's post-9/11 terrorist crackdown. Under questioning, captured al-Qaeda operatives described bin Laden's preferred mode of communication. Not trusting electronics, he passed his orders through letters hand-carried by fanatically devoted couriers. One in particular caught the CIA's attention, though he was known only by a nickname. Interrogators grilled 9/11 mastermind Khalid Sheikh Mohammed for details about him. When he pleaded ignorance, they knew they were onto something promising. Abu Faraj al-Libbi, a senior al-Qaeda figure captured in 2005, also played dumb. Both men were subjected to so-called enhanced interrogation techniques, including, in Mohammed's case, the waterboard. The U.S. previously prosecuted as torturers those who used waterboarding, and critics say it violates international treaties. They also argue that extreme techniques are counterproductive. The report that Mohammed and al-Libbi were more forthcoming after the harsh treatment guarantees that the argument will go on.

The U.S. had finally found the long-sought needle in a huge and dangerous haystack

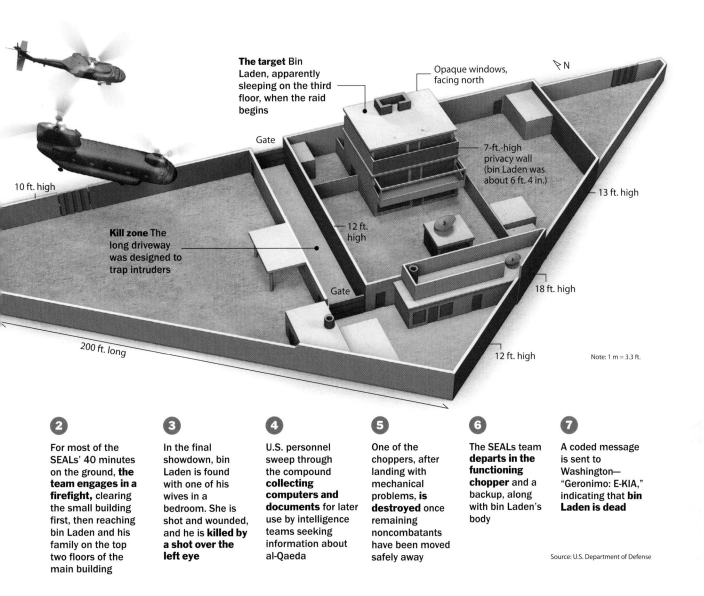

Gradually, the courier's identity was pieced together. The next job was to find him. In the summer of 2010, agents intercepted the call they'd been waiting for. CIA agents had picked up the courier's trail in Peshawar and then followed him until he led them to the unusual compound in Abbottabad. Now the National Geospatial-Intelligence Agency trained a spy satellite on the triangular fortress. Over time, despite the residents' secrecy, U.S. analysts grew more confident that they had finally hit the jackpot.

Obama was first informed of the breakthrough in August. By February the clues were solid enough for CIA Director Leon Panetta to begin planning a raid. "I don't want you to plan for an option that doesn't allow you to fight your way out," Obama told his military planners. Darkness was the cloak, and speed essential; the soldiers had to be in and out of Pakistan before its military could respond. They rehearsed against a 30-minute clock. The orders were to capture or take out al-Qaeda's leader.

When the decision was made to strike the compound, bin Laden still had not been spotted among the residents behind the walls. The raiders found him near the end of their search through the house. The courier was already dead on the first floor, along with his brother and a woman caught in the cross fire. When the SEALs encountered bin Laden, he was with one of his wives. The young woman started toward the SEALs and was shot in the leg. Bin Laden, unarmed, appeared ready to resist, according to a Defense Department account.

In an instant it was over: in all, four men and one woman lay dead. Bin Laden was shot in the head and in the chest. One of bin Laden's wives confirmed his identity even as a photograph of the dead man's face was dispatched to a face-recognition program. As the SEAL team prepared to load the body onto a helicopter, a senior military officer at CIA headquarters delivered the verdict, relayed to the White House Situation Room: "Geronimo: E-KIA," meaning Enemy—killed in action.

"We got him," Obama said.

The strike force had eluded Pakistani radar on the flight into the country, but once the firefight erupted, the air force scrambled jets, which might arrive with guns blazing. A decision was made to destroy the stricken chopper. In the meantime, SEALs emerged from the house carrying computer drives and other potential intelligence treasures collected during a hasty search.

Aloft, the raiders performed a head count to confirm that they hadn't lost a man during the mission. DNA from the body was matched to known relatives of bin Laden's—a third form of identification.

The dead man's next stop was the U.S.S. *Carl Vinson,* an aircraft carrier in the Arabian Sea. There, his body was washed per Islamic law, wrapped in a white sheet, then dropped overboard. There would be no grave for his admirers to venerate. The face that haunted the Western world, the eyes that looked on the blazing towers with pride, sank sightless beneath the waves. ■

—By David Von Drehle

MICHAEL APPLETON—THE NEW YORK TIMES—REDUX PICUTRES

Full circle *Firefighters gather in New York City's Times Square late on the evening of May 1 as the news breaks that Osama bin Laden has been killed in Pakistan. On Sept. 11, 2001, 343 of their colleagues died in the attack on the World Trade Center*

Osama bin Laden. His path to a fanatic's death

Osama bin Laden was not born to the role of terrorist ringleader. He wasn't brilliant. He didn't give great speeches. He was not charismatic. Bin Laden's life—and the strong personalities to which the impressionable and fatherless young man was exposed—took him to the outermost extreme, one graduated step at a time. He was born in 1957 to a Syrian mother and a Yemen-born father, Mohammed bin Laden, who had immigrated to Jidda, Saudi Arabia, established a construction business, befriended King Abdul Aziz ibn Saud and become wealthy. With his 22 wives—never more than four at a time, per Islamic law—Mohammed had 54 children. Osama was born somewhere in the middle.

When bin Laden was 10, his father, whom he worshipped, died in a plane crash. His mother married another Jidda businessman, with whom she had more children, and she and Osama moved out of the bin Laden compound. At 19 he married his first cousin Najwa, 13. Such unions are not uncommon in the Arab world. The seeds of fanaticism began to sprout when he attended college in Jidda, where he first met Abdullah Azzam, 16 years his senior. The Palestinian radical hoped to unite the entire Muslim world in a pure Islamic state through holy war.

When the Soviet Union invaded Afghanistan in 1979, Azzam sped to the front to help the rebel Afghans known as the mujahedin. Bin Laden dropped out of school and followed Azzam. In Peshawar, they ran an agency that assisted the Arab volunteers joining the mujahedin. Eventually, bin Laden fought in Afghanistan, winning acclaim for his leadership and bravery; his troops began calling him "the Sheik." Despite his privileged background, he slept with his men on floors and shared their simple meals. Yet he also began to dabble in self-promotion, hiring an Egyptian journalist to film and write about his exploits.

When the Soviets withdrew from Afghanistan, bin Laden began drifting out of Azzam's orbit and into that of the more fanatical Ayman al-Zawahiri, an Egyptian physician and a leader of al-Jihad, the group behind the 1981 assassination of Egyptian President Anwar Sadat. Returning to Saudi Arabia, bin Laden was received as a national hero for his exploits in Afghanistan. He began calling for worldwide jihad and organizing Arab veterans of the Afghan war to fight against the Marxist regime of South Yemen next door, an ally of the Saudi regime, which yanked his passport so that he could no longer travel abroad.

After Iraq invaded Kuwait in 1990, the Saudi government invited U.S. forces to establish a presence there, which infuriated bin Laden. Now persona non grata in Saudi Arabia, he made his way to Sudan, then experimenting with Islamic rule. In a wealthy suburb of Khartoum, he rented a house of three stories, one for each of the wives he had by then acquired. He quickly won government construction contracts, but he stayed so close to the violent anti-Western groups forming in Sudan that the Saudi government, a U.S. ally, stripped him of his citizenship.

Mujahedin *Fighting Soviets in Afghanistan in the late 1980s*

AAR—SIPA PRESS

By 1995, the U.S. linked him to the ringleader of the 1993 World Trade Center attack and to a plot to murder Egyptian President Hosni Mubarak in Ethiopia, and he was now a wanted man. Pressed by the U.S. and Egypt, Sudan asked bin Laden to leave. He flew into Jalalabad by chartered plane with an entourage of lieutenants, wives and children and began turning Afghanistan into headquarters for a worldwide jihad. By the end of 1996, it had become the best possible base for bin Laden. The Taliban, led by a scarcely educated cleric, Mullah Mohammed Omar, had taken control of Kabul. Bin Laden became his mentor.

In August 1998 al-Qaeda operatives bombed U.S. embassies in Kenya and Tanzania, killing 224 people, mostly Africans. Washington retaliated with a cruise-missile attack on Afghanistan that narrowly missed bin Laden. Al-Qaeda struck again in 2000, attacking the U.S.S. *Cole* in Yemen and killing 17 U.S. service members. Then came Sept. 11 and the start of the war against terrorism.

In what was apparently bin Laden's last interview, with a Pakistani journalist on Nov. 7, 2001, in a secret hideout outside Kabul, the terrorist was asked if he would surrender if he became trapped. He laughed and replied, "I am a person who loves death. The Americans love life. I will engage them and fight. I will not surrender. If I am to die, I would like to be killed by the bullet." On May 1, 2011, in Pakistan, U.S. Navy SEALs obliged him.

NATION

A Decade of Grief. Ten years on, Americans remember 9/11

A few months after the Sept. 11, 2001, attack on the World Trade Center that brought down its Twin Towers, Rudolph Giuliani, then the outgoing mayor of New York City, called for a "soaring" memorial to the people who died at Ground Zero. But 10 years later, TIME architecture critic Richard Lacayo observed, as the completed memorial was dedicated at last, "[it] carries us in the opposite direction. Two massive square voids sited within the footprints of the towers, it digs down—almost as if the collapse of the towers had pounded out a space to deposit feelings about that whole wretched day."

Horrified and anguished by the attack on their nation, Americans have struggled in the past decade to find appropriate spaces in which to deposit their feelings. But after long, frustrating delays, two new memorials were opened on the 10th anniversary of the attacks. Lacayo judged the new National 9/11 Memorial at the World Trade Center a splendid monument: "If there's one lesson it offers," he wrote, "it's that there's more than one way to soar." Meanwhile, the National Park Service opened a new, permanent memorial in Shanksville, Pa., that honors the passengers and crew of United Flight 93, while the memorial site at the Pentagon in Washington observed its third anniversary on Sept. 11. ■

LEFT: POLARIS; RIGHT, FROM TOP: MANDEL NGAN—AFP—GETTY IMAGES; BRENDAN SMIALOWSKI—GETTY IMAGES

The World Trade Center

Former President George W. Bush and wife Laura joined President Barack Obama and First Lady Michelle Obama in the day's major memorial service, held at the World Trade Center site in lower Manhattan, left. Plans for the rebuilding of the site languished for years amid political battles and funding disputes, but most of the memorial is complete and construction on the transit hub and main office tower are now moving forward.

The National 9/11 Memorial was formally opened on Sept. 11. Two massive square voids are sited within the footprints of the Twin Towers that fell here. On all four sides of each void, waterfalls descend into a broad reflecting pool. At ground level, the names of all the Americans who died in the 9/11 attacks (and in the 1993 bombing at the World Trade Center) are engraved—cut all the way through, actually, and backlit at night—on bronze panels along the parapets that form the perimeter of each void.

Shanksville, Pa.

President Obama and the First Lady placed a wreath in front of a new memorial wall, above, that features the names of the 40 Americans who died aboard United Airlines Flight 93 on 9/11/01. Former Presidents Bill Clinton and George W. Bush also attended the ceremonies.

The jetliner crashed in Shanksville, Pa., after passengers fought back against four terrorists who had hijacked it and hoped to crash it in Washington. The day marked the opening of a 1,500-acre park at the site, operated by the National Park Service, though it is unfinished. More than 1 million people have visited the site in the past 10 years.

The Pentagon

The Pentagon Memorial, which opened on Sept. 11, 2008, honors the 184 Americans who were killed when American Airlines Flight 77 plowed into the west side of the nation's military headquarters on 9/11/01. The site features 184 illuminated benches, left, each dedicated to a victim of the attack.

On Sept. 11, Vice President Joe Biden joined Defense Secretary Leon Panetta and Navy Admiral Mike Mullen, chairman of the Joint Chiefs of Staff, in a morning memorial service at the site. President Obama and the First Lady visited the site later in the day and placed a memorial wreath to honor the fallen.

In Brief

A New Memorial Honors Dr. King's Legacy

WASHINGTON In his lifetime, Martin Luther King Jr. wasn't stopped by water cannons or police dogs. But Hurricane Irene put a damper on the dedication of the new Martin Luther King Jr. National Memorial in Washington, postponing it from Aug. 28 to Oct. 16. The memorial takes its shape from a phrase in King's 1963 clarion call for justice, the "I Have a Dream" speech: "With this faith we will be able to hew out of the mountain of despair a stone of hope." The memorial divides the Mountain of Despair into two 30-ft. (9 m) -high masses of carved granite that face each other across a divide. Viewers walk between them and emerge onto a plaza to find the Stone of Hope, a giant figure of King sculpted by Chinese artist Lei Yixin, emerging from the rough granite. Behind it is a long wall inscribed with King quotations.

TIME architecture critic Richard Lacayo praised the memorial, the work of San Francisco's Roma Design Group, writing, "[It] is the most effective monument to appear in Washington since Maya Lin's brilliant reinvention of the form in 1982 in the Vietnam Veterans Memorial. As a work of art, the stiffly modeled sculpture of King at its center has its problems. But as a work of visual rhetoric, a device for summoning feelings about one of the greatest Americans, the first monument on the National Mall devoted to a man who was never President—and the first for an African American—gets a lot of things right."

"I think that the Republican Party would be well advised to get the heck out of people's bedrooms."

RUDOLPH GIULIANI, former mayor of New York City and TIME's Person of the Year 2001, commenting on his party's stance on gay marriage in New York State

More Milestones For U.S. Gays

ALBANY, N.Y. When New York's state senate passed a bill on June 24 making gay marriage legal in the state, 33-to-29, cheers of "U.S.A.! U.S.A.!" erupted in the chamber. The historic vote followed an 80-to-63 vote in the state assembly the week before and made the Empire State the sixth to allow same-sex marriage. Below, newlyweds celebrate after marrying under the new law.

On Sept. 20, the military's policy forbidding openly gay service members, widely known as "Don't ask, don't tell" (DADT), was officially retired. The new policy followed a December 2010 congressional vote to repeal DADT, as well as a July 2011 ruling by a three-judge U.S. federal appeals panel that DADT was unconstitutional. The White House and Joint Chiefs of Staff supported the changes.

FROM LEFT: EVAN GOLUB—DEMOTIX—CORBIS; JIM LEE—BLOOMBERG VIA GETTY IMAGES

At Arlington National Cemetery, a Search for Missing Heroes

ARLINGTON, VA. *The scandals at the nation's foremost military cemetery, Arlington, surfaced in 2010, when it was revealed that the locations of hundreds of grave sites were either incorrect or unknown. As* TIME'*s Mark Benjamin revealed in 2011, the U.S. Army first learned of the problems in 1992, then again in 1997—but took only halting steps to resolve them. Arlington's superintendent and chief deputy were replaced in 2010, but cemetery officials are still tracking the locations of some 30 burials a day on scraps of paper.*

Exit Frying Pan, Enter Fire

CHICAGO When Richard Daley declared in September 2010 that he would step down as mayor of Chicago after 21 years in office, White House chief of staff Rahm Emanuel heard the starter's bell. The famously brash, constantly driven and frequently vulgar policy wonk, a Chicago native and vocal booster, quickly assembled a team of political experts, raised $12 million in three months, triumphed against a legal charge that he did not meet residence requirements—and won the Feb. 22 election with 55% of the vote. Said the Windy City's new boss, 52: "Every city faces ... challenges. I want to be the first to solve them."

NUMBERS

64

Number of years since not a single member of the Kennedy family was serving as an elected official in Washington, after Representative Patrick Kennedy left the House on Jan. 3, 2011

3,366

Number of U.S. soldiers injured by improvised explosive devices in Afghanistan in 2010—a 178% increase over the number in 2009

Disaster at the Air Show

RENO, NEV. In the deadliest incident at an air show in decades, 11 people died and almost 70 were injured when a vintage World War II airplane, the heavily remodeled P-51 Mustang christened the "Galloping Ghost," lost altitude and plunged into a seating area in the grandstand at the annual Reno Air Races. Veteran stunt pilot Jimmy Leeward, 74, died in the crash. The air show, the last in the U.S. to feature actual racing, has come under fire in the past for lax safety regulations; 20 pilots have died there since the event began in 1964.

TOP: KEVIN WOLF—AP IMAGES. BOTTOM, FROM LEFT: KIICHIRO SATA—AP IMAGES; WARD HOWES—AP IMAGES

World

A boy in the newly independent nation of
South Sudan faces the future on July 9

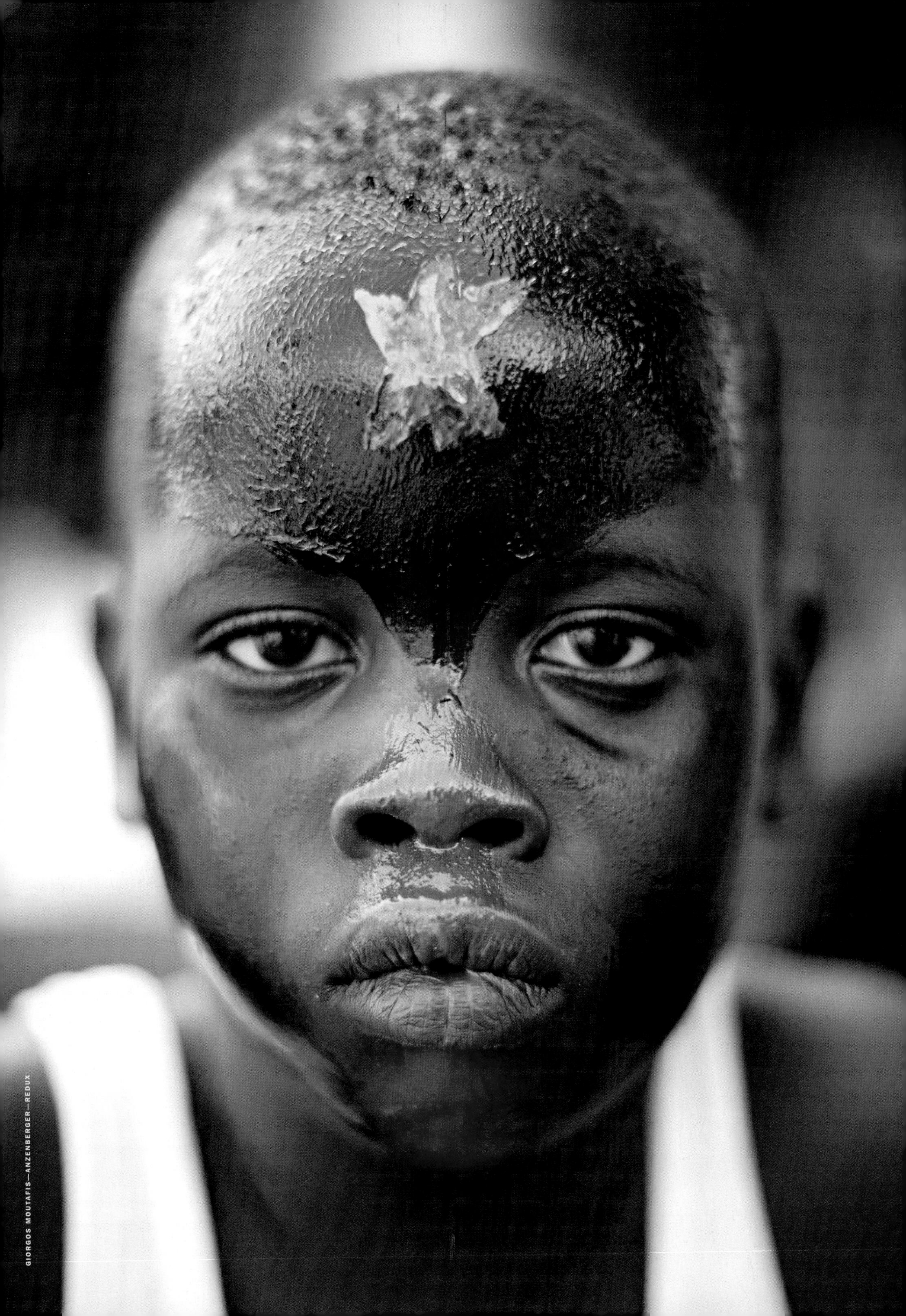

GIORGOS MOUTAFIS—ANZENBERGER—REDUX

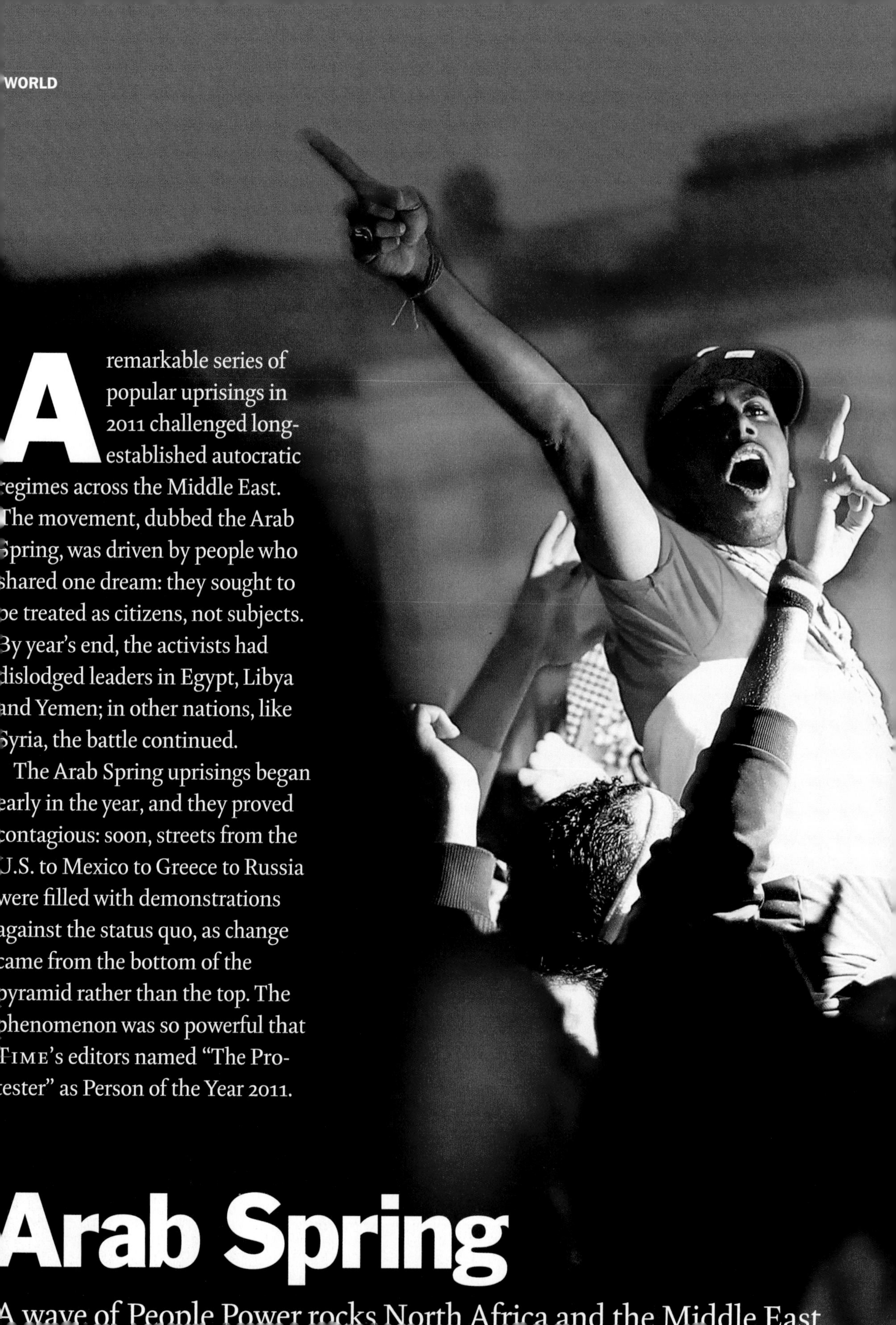

A remarkable series of popular uprisings in 2011 challenged long-established autocratic regimes across the Middle East. The movement, dubbed the Arab Spring, was driven by people who shared one dream: they sought to be treated as citizens, not subjects. By year's end, the activists had dislodged leaders in Egypt, Libya and Yemen; in other nations, like Syria, the battle continued.

The Arab Spring uprisings began early in the year, and they proved contagious: soon, streets from the U.S. to Mexico to Greece to Russia were filled with demonstrations against the status quo, as change came from the bottom of the pyramid rather than the top. The phenomenon was so powerful that TIME's editors named "The Protester" as Person of the Year 2011.

Arab Spring

A wave of People Power rocks North Africa and the Middle East

JOHN MOORE—GETTY IMAGES

Feb. 11 *Egyptians celebrate in Cairo's Tahrir Square after hearing that President Mubarak would voluntarily step down*

Tunisia. A martyr's self-immolation jump-starts a revolution

No bomb exploded to announce the start of Tunisia's Jasmine Revolution, and in the end, there was no iconic figure—no Nelson Mandela or Vaclav Havel—to declare its stunning victory. Instead, the fuse for the Arab world's first successful popular uprising was lit when a Tunisian policewoman in the small town of Sidi Bouzid slapped a fruit seller on Dec. 17, 2010. A trivial incident, but what happened next went viral, unleashing the seething frustrations of a generation of Tunisians raised under a sclerotic dictatorship.

The fruit seller was computer-science graduate Mohammed Bouazizi, 26. Unable to find work as a computer technician, he sold fruit to support his seven siblings, and the slap was one humiliation too many. He marched to the governor's office and demanded an appointment, threatening to set himself alight if the official did not meet him. Turned away, Bouazizi carried out his macabre threat. With his death 18 days later, millions of angry young Tunisians had a martyr. Their frustration had been mounting in recent years as the unwritten compact their parents' generation had made with President Zine el Abidine Ben Ali—more economic opportunity in exchange for fewer political freedoms—had come undone. Recently, unemployment and inflation had soared, and the regime had become ever more corrupt.

Bouazizi's cause was taken up by Tunisia's wildly popular rapper El Général, whose song *Rais Elbled* ("President of the Republic") became the protesters' anthem. Its enraged lyrics prompted the government to ban YouTube in a futile attempt to quell the protests. The revolt surged from town to town, fueled by a steady stream of anonymous text messages, Twitter and Facebook updates; within four weeks, it engulfed Tunis. On Jan. 13, Ben Ali, 75, appeared on state television and offered to give up power in 2014, when the next presidential election was due. But his 10.5 million subjects already sensed that liberation was at hand. The next morning, "We went on air and said, 'The dictatorship is over,'" recalled Noureddine Boutan, director of the nation's biggest music station, which had never dared to criticize the President. Within hours, Ben Ali fled the country, leaving behind a nation in turmoil. Soon Prime Minister Mohammed Ghannouchi also stepped down; a new PM, Beji Caid-Essebsi, was named; and elections for a constituent assembly were scheduled for late October.

Jan. 26 *Protesters gather near the office of Prime Minister Ghannouchi, who was later displaced in the revolution*

CAPUCINE BAILLY—REDUX

Feb. 11 *Army tanks in Cairo's Tahrir Square are surrounded by protesters in the hours before President Mubarak declared he would leave office. The military took the people's side during the crisis*

KUNI TAKAHASHI—POLARIS

Egypt. A longtime leader steps down, but the military holds the reins

Egyptians have long been seen as a people deferential to authority; in the popular imagination, they are passive, meekly submitting to religion and hierarchy. But at the end of January 2011, the streets of Cairo and Alexandria and other cities were filled with a different people: crowds of energetic, strong-willed men from all walks of life and even some women, all determined to shape their own destiny. The center of Egypt's swirling political vortex was Cairo's Tahrir Square, where Egyptians of many ages and faiths could be seen smiling and laughing, waving witty banners, organizing spontaneous soccer tournaments and thrusting cigarettes and flowers into the hands of longtime President Hosni Mubarak's surprisingly sympathetic soldiers.

The protests began on Jan. 25, at the urging of a Facebook page later found to have been created by a young Egyptian Google executive living in Dubai, Wael Ghonim, 30. The joy in the gatherings was contagious, but everyone knew the reverie might end. The attempted clampdown came on Feb. 2, when armed pro-Mubarak forces confronted the protesters with rocks and machetes and Molotov cocktails, even camels. The rearguard action by Mubarak's thugs felt like the final death spasm of a dictatorship. And it was. On Feb. 11, Mubarak, the nation's strongman since 1981, said he would step down.

Within months, Egyptians gathered again in Tahrir Square to watch the televised trial of Mubarak, 83, ailing and confined to a stretcher, as he defended himself against charges of murdering protesters. But by the fall, the events of February came to seem more like a military coup than a revolution, as generals kept a tight grasp on power, squelching liberal dreams. On Nov. 18, 10 days before voting was to begin for a fresh parliament that would draft a new constitution, Tahrir Square again came alive with protests. This time the people clashed violently with police, who sided with the military. Amid a huge turnout, the Islamist party the Muslim Brotherhood was outpacing other parties in the elections, with full results not expected until after the new year. But the question remained: Would the army give up power?

Feb. 18 *Citizens of Bahrain show their support for King Hamad and the minority Sunni regime*

Bahrain. The King strikes back

When the surging wave of protests hit tiny, oil-rich Bahrain, People Power proved no match for a tough autocracy. Peaceful marches began in the capital, Manama, in February, as protesters, mainly from the nation's indigenous Shi'ite majority, called for a constitutional monarchy. Bahrain's Shi'ites have long complained of marginalization at the hands of the minority Sunni dynasty in power. But King Hamad bin Isa al-Khalifa, 61, a Sunni, held firm and appealed for aid to Bahrain's powerful neighbors. On March 14, 1,000 Saudi Arabian troops and 500 police officers from the United Arab Emirates entered Manama.

The clampdown was brutal: more than 30 people were killed, and some 500 demonstrators were swept up by the state's security forces. In March, a military court sentenced four Shi'ite men to death for allegedly killing two police officers during the protests. Countering state propaganda, activists said the uprisings had little to do with Muslim sectarian divisions and far more with popular demands for political reform. Iran, the Shi'ite power in the Middle East and the Saudis' longtime enemy, denounced the regime's actions.

Yemen. Longtime President Saleh is wounded and steps down

As in Bahrain, protests in Yemen early in the year turned into violent clashes between forces loyal to embattled President Ali Abdullah Saleh, right, and those calling for an immediate end to his long rule. The fighting was most intense around the main university campus in the capital, Sana'a, and in the port city of Aden. A host of tribal and factional rebellions simmered in the fractious nation, a U.S. ally.

Saleh took a tough stand, but with support for the leader eroding among the military and key local tribes, Washington urged him to step down. The President, 69, in office since 1978, refused to do so. On June 3, his compound was rocked by an explosion, and a badly burned Saleh was taken to Saudi Arabia for treatment. Vice President Abd al-Rab Mansur al-Hadi became acting President, though Saleh's son and relatives remained power brokers. On Nov. 23, under great internal and external pressure, Saleh signed a transition plan, brokered by the Gulf Cooperation Council, a political union of Arab states, under which he immediately stepped down and formally transferred power to al-Hadi, who began forming a national unity government.

March 24 *Their faces adorned with the signs of their revolt, young protesters in Yemen's capital city, Sana'a, demand the resignation of President Ali Abdullah Saleh*

CLOCKWISE FROM TOP LEFT: RICK LOOMIS—LOS ANGELES TIMES—POLARIS; JONATHAN SARUK—GETTY IMAGES; YIN KEXINHUA—POLARIS

April 28 *Antigovernment protesters rally in the streets in Nawa, near Dara'a, southern epicenter of the uprising that rocked the nation throughout the year and brought a deadly response from the repressive Assad regime*

Syria. A brutal government goes to war against its citizens

Protests against the government of President Bashar Assad, 46, who took power after his father Hafez Assad's death in 2000, were inspired by the revolutions in Egypt and Tunisia. Demonstrators represented the Sunni majority as well as a Shi'ite minority known as the Alawites, which provides much of the country's ruling class. But Syria is not Egypt: the government's violent response to the protests was typical of a deeply entrenched regime that has consolidated power through terrorism, collective punishment, mass detentions and the oppression of intellectuals and politicians for the past 48 years. A brute intolerance of opposition has long been the Assads' hallmark: when Islamists in the city of Hama rose in protest against the government in 1982, security forces shelled the town, killing anywhere from 10,000 to 40,000 civilians.

The protests began in earnest in early March, and the government quickly reacted, as tanks and soldiers stormed large rallies in such cities as Dara'a, Hama and Hams. Some Syrian soldiers who refused to fire on civilians were reportedly shot by their own officers, and the government cut off the water and electricity in some cities. The Assad regime continued to command support in the nation's two largest cities, Aleppo and Damascus. In July, pro-government forces attacked the U.S. and French embassies in Damascus, after the Western nations expressed support for the uprising.

The violence never let up, as a deeply divided nation drifted into outright civil war. As of December, rights organizations were estimating that somewhere between 5,000 and 6,000 Syrians had died in the rebellion, counting both civilians and government forces. President Assad clung to power, weathering economic sanctions imposed by Western nations, calls by the U.S. and Turkey for him to step down, and the expulsion of Syria from the Arab League by member nations.

As TIME's Rania Abouzeid reported in late August, government posters all around Damascus read, SYRIA IS FINE. But Syria was not fine, the uprising was far from over, and the future promised more violence to come.

AFP—GETTY IMAGES

معك نعانق
المجد

Libya. With NATO aid, rebels bring down a dictator

There's more than one way to topple a tyrant. The largely peaceful protests that took down dictators in Tunis and Cairo weren't employed in Libya, where a ragtag army of rebels sought to force longtime strongman Muammar Gaddafi, 69, from power. Their path wouldn't be viral: the Berber guerrillas of the Nafusa Mountains didn't pause to set up Facebook pages as they swept into the plains south and west of Tripoli. It wouldn't be telegenic: the rebel leaders in Benghazi could find no Libyan Wael Ghonim to articulate their aspirations for a global TV audience. It would be very bloody: estimates of the death toll from six months of seesaw battles range from 9,000 to 15,000. And it wouldn't be entirely an Arab effort, because NATO bombers and drones would play a key part.

No matter: it worked. In a campaign that lasted from March until late October, the rebels, with a strong assist from NATO, brought down the Gaddafi regime, and the dictator was killed. United under the banner of the National Transitional Council (NTC), the rebels were led by Mahmoud Jibril, a political scientist respected throughout the Middle East, who acted as the de facto Prime Minister, and Mustafa Abdul-Jalil, a former Justice Minister. The two managed to maintain a degree of law and order in Benghazi, their base, and urged their fighters to be restrained and responsible, especially in their treatment of Gaddafi loyalists, although international monitoring agencies reported instances of rebel atrocities throughout the campaign. Despite the assassination of their top general, Abdel Fattah Younes, on July 28, the rebels remained largely united and focused. Their leaders overcame international reservations and eventually won acceptance for the NTC as Libya's unofficial government, certified by the U.N. during its General Assembly session in New York City in September.

The rebels' victory was also a big win for the Obama Administration. The President startled Americans when he declared that the U.S. would aid their cause through NATO. The intervention was criticized by voices on both the left and the right, but Obama held firm. A NATO coalition led by U.S., British and French forces launched air strikes against Gaddafi loyalists besieging Benghazi on March 19 and began to enforce a no-fly zone authorized by the U.N. Security Council. Both the air raids and the arms and matériel supplied to rebel troops initially seemed ineffective. They began to pay off early in August, when the rebels launched the campaign along the northern coast that met surprisingly little resistance.

The rebels swept into Tripoli's iconic Green Square on Aug. 21. Within days, they had taken control of Gaddafi's fortified compound, and he and his remaining loyalists fled to Sirt, his hometown and last stronghold, some 230 miles (370 km) east of Tripoli. The loyalists put up a tough fight in the coastal city, but on Oct. 20 their resistance collapsed, and amid the fighting, Gaddafi was found cowering in a sewage pipe, apparently after his escape convoy was hit by fire from a NATO jet or helicopter, which killed many if not most of his escort.

The events that followed are not clear. On cell-phone video posted on YouTube and then broadcast worldwide, Gaddafi is seen being captured alive, surrounded by enraged Libyans hitting him. He then appears to have been dragged to a vehicle and driven away. Jibril told TIME in an interview the evening of the events that Gaddafi was accidentally caught in a fierce firefight between his supporters and fighters of the new regime. "There was cross fire, and he was shot while they [rebels] were carrying him to a truck," he said.

If those details are correct, it would mean that the rebel fighters intended to take Gaddafi alive. That would have adhered to the wishes of Western governments, which had expressed the hope that he would be tried in an international court. The U.N. and many Western nations called for an investigation into the dictator's death. But to the hundreds of thousands of Libyans who were celebrating the end of 42 years of Gaddafi's harsh, murderous rule, the details of his demise seemed almost an afterthought. Revenge was in the air: Gaddafi's bloodied and beaten corpse was laid out for days in the cold-storage room of a food market in Misratah, between Sirt and Tripoli, and thousands of people lined up to view it.

Going forward, Libya faces familiar concerns: tribal, ethnic or racial war could break out; the rebel leadership lacks figures of national appeal; the country, long led by one man with an iron will, has weak, unreliable institutions. The future may be cloudy, but few Libyans regret that Muammar Gaddafi will not be part of it. ■

Up in smoke *A poster of Gaddafi burns in Benghazi, the rebels' western stronghold, in March*

Is Palestine Ready for Statehood?

Mahmoud Abbas pleads his cause on the world's biggest stage

As world leaders gathered in New York City in mid-September for the annual talkfest that is the U.N. General Assembly, the hottest topic of conversation was a bold move by Palestinian National Authority President Mahmoud Abbas: an appeal to the U.N. to recognize his people's territories as an independent nation. The Palestinians said this was their best hope of restarting stalled peace talks with Israel, but the hard-line government of Israeli Prime Minister Benjamin Netanyahu denounced the plan, saying statehood could only follow the negotiation of a peace plan between the two warring entities in those talks. Chicken, meet egg.

On Sept. 23, Abbas presented his plan to the General Assembly. The reaction was swift: the U.S. urged the resumption of talks, while most U.N. nations endorsed the plan. Netanyahu's response was the firmest: on Sept. 27, his government announced the building of 1,100 new homes in the disputed Gilo area of East Jerusalem. Such new settlements are the roadblock holding up further talks: every government in the world except Israel's regards them as illegal, as well as a huge physical obstacle to peace.

As TIME's Tony Karon observed, Abbas had apparently concluded that the current "peace process," managed by Washington for two decades, has become an integral part of the status quo, providing political and diplomatic cover for the ongoing expansion of Israel's occupation of Palestinian territory and offering no prospect for ending it. By going to the U.N., Abbas was calling for the matter to be taken out of the hands of the U.S., where, he believes, wide support for Israel precludes the nation from serving as an honest broker in the region. Indeed, on Oct. 3, Palestinians announced that millions of dollars pledged to aid development projects in the West Bank had been frozen by U.S. congressional committees, as a rebuke to Abbas.

After the U.N. meetings, Abbas launched a world tour to drum up support for his plan. On Oct. 18, as he was on the road, Israel released more than 1,000 Palestinian political prisoners in exchange for Gilad Shalit, the Israeli soldier captured by Hamas in 2006, at age 19, whose detention has long been a cause célèbre in Israel. It was a rare moment of optimism in a region starved for compromise. (It was also a rebuke to Abbas, the political foe of Hamas.) But welcome as the successful Israel-Hamas prisoner exchange was, it was not a peace treaty, it was not independence for Palestine, and it did not promise to end the decades-long duel between two bitter foes. ■

Man of the hour *At left, Palestinians in Ramallah in the West Bank wave posters celebrating leader Mahmoud Abbas in September. On Oct. 31, the U.N. social and cultural agency UNESCO voted 107 to 14, with 52 abstentions, to admit Palestine as a full member. The decision will cost the agency one-fourth of its annual budget, which is donated by the U.S. (22%) and Israel (3%)*

MEHDI CHEBIL—POLARIS

The riot act *London police form a cordon as parts of the city go up in flames*

London Burning: Anarchy in the U.K.

Riots plague Britain's cities, as a divided nation reels in shock

THE EYES OF THE WORLD FOCUSED ON BRITAIN early in August, as London, Manchester, Birmingham and other cities were torched and ransacked in four nights of mayhem after the police killing of a North Londoner named Mark Duggan. When order was finally restored, Prime Minister David Cameron, who cut short a Tuscan holiday to return and face the crisis, offered his view: "This is criminality, pure and simple." Photos and videotape would seem to back him up: the hooded arsonists, looters and brick heavers seemed much keener on destruction and theft than on political reform.

The authorities saw the rioters as amoral outliers. "We want to make it absolutely clear: they have nothing to protest against," said a Manchester police official. Really? In 2005 (the most recent year for which data exist) nearly 30% of income in the U.K. went to the top 5% of earners. And Britain still labors under the class system, with scant social mobility for most. The unemployment rate for people ages 16 to 24 rose from 14% to 20% in recent years. And yet when the Cameron government looked to slash the budget in a down economy, the ax seemed to fall heaviest on the very people who were hurting the most.

Nor was the looting racially motivated. Duggan was black, and there are strong correlations between race and class in Britain. But some of the worst violence happened in majority-white neighborhoods. The riots were fueled not by race but by economic and social inequality.

A few of the rioters blamed Cameron. But some of the disaffection with his team has more to do with the people around him than their policies. The Prime Minister was educated at Eton and Oxford; his deputy, Nick Clegg, at Westminster and Cambridge; and so on. The Cameron Cabinet represents the very oldest notions of a British élite, at a time when the U.K. is more diverse than ever.

Only months after the riots struck Britain, major cities around the world also swarmed with protests. Perhaps history will see the Arab Spring, Britain's riots and the Occupy Wall Street movement as manifestations of a period when long-hidden social discontents were brought to the light of day—if, sometimes, in criminal form. ■

DAN ISTITENE—GETTY IMAGES

PROFILE

Ai Weiwei

China's foremost artist is a challenge to a regime deeply wary of a free spirit

CHINA'S BEST-KNOWN MODERN artist, Ai Weiwei, 54, is a burly online oversharer with 78,000 followers on Twitter. His artworks mine history and politics in provocative ways, and he has a global following. In the spring of 2011, his new work was on view at both London's Tate Modern museum and New York City's Central Park.

But Ai is more than an artist. The son of Ai Qing, a beloved revolutionary poet, Ai has emerged as one of the most prominent critics of China's ruling Communist Party, drawing public focus to some of his nation's most tragic recent events, including the government's cover-up of the number and causes of deaths in the 2008 earthquake in Sichuan that killed some 6,000 children. He also brought public attention to other instances of possible corruption, including the murder of a village chief in Zhejiang in which he suspects authorities may have been involved.

Ai, in short, spelled trouble for China's regime, which is due to change at the top in 2012. On April 3, amid a nationwide crackdown on dissent, he was stopped while attempting to board a flight to Hong Kong and was detained with little explanation by authorities. A worldwide outcry followed. Ai was finally released on June 22, after 81 days of detention, during which he was held in a 12-ft. by 24-ft. (3.6 m by 7.2 m) room, watched at all times by two military police and interrogated 50 times.

Once released, Ai kept mum for a spell, but the artist was soon back on Twitter, again questioning the regime "I will never stop fighting injustice," he declared. ■

SHIHI FUKADA—THE NEW YORK TIMES—REDUX

Egypt's new face *After Mubarak's resignation, a smiling Ghonim, center, relaxed in a Cairo café*

PROFILE

Wael Ghonim

The revolution he helped lead wasn't televised. It was tweeted

TALKATIVE, ENERGETIC AND CONFIDENT, Wael Ghonim is just like many in the new generation of Arabs who are out to change their world—and prosper in it—by way of technology. "We live in a digital age, and it is important that the Arab world take advantage of this new medium," the young Egyptian once told an Abu Dhabi paper.

Slim and standing a little more than average height, Ghonim, 30, is typical of the new guard: he speaks English with an American accent but is audibly Arab when he pronounces Arabic words. He is at ease in both worlds: in recent years the expatriate Egyptian lived in Dubai and worked as Google's head of marketing for the Middle East and North Africa.

But in spite of his comfortable life, Ghonim chose to be part of a hidden, more dangerous world—one in which he sought to activate change in his homeland. Only a few of Ghonim's friends knew that he was the creator of the Facebook page "We Are All Khaled Said" in 2010, on which he called for the Jan. 25, 2011, uprising in Tahrir Square. (Said was a 28-year-old techie and businessman who is believed to have been brutally killed by police in Alexandria in 2010.)

In January 2011, Ghonim returned to Egypt from Dubai, telling his colleagues he was visiting his native country to resolve a "personal problem." When the protests began, on his timetable, he was in the thick of the action. On Jan. 27, Ghonim tweeted, "Pray for Egypt. Very worried as it seems that government is planning a war crime tomorrow against people. We are all ready to die." He was arrested soon afterward; upon his release, 10 days later, he appeared in Tahrir Square, where he was hailed by the crowd. A reluctant hero, Ghonim credits the people of Egypt with forcing President Hosni Mubarak's Feb. 11 resignation. Once ready to die, Egyptians are now ready to live. ■

MARTIN SCHOELLER—AUGUST

Newlyweds *Prince William and the former Kate Middleton—named the Duke and Duchess of Cambridge earlier on their wedding day—emerge from Westminster Abbey, all smiles*

MARTIN MEISSNER—AP IMAGES

WORLD

The Masters Of Majesty

A Prince marries a commoner, as Britain's House of Windsor looks to the future

HAD LONDON BEEN A SHIP, SHE MIGHT HAVE LISTED. DAYS BEFORE the wedding of His Royal Highness Prince William Arthur Philip Louis and Catherine Elizabeth Middleton, it began: the inexorable buildup of spectators along the ceremonial route, at first a straggle of flag-bedecked diehards, then the crowds and finally hordes, all intent on squeezing into the same small corner of a sprawling city. Some were locals, but many had traveled across countries and continents. Those lucky or determined enough to grab the best vantage points caught fleeting glimpses of oxblood-colored Rolls-Royces and open carriages and their smartly dressed occupants. The greater press of people, their views obscured, raised smartphones like periscopes. What mattered was not seeing the pageantry but living it.

You can understand why Britons and citizens of the 54 nations of the Commonwealth would take more than a passing interest in an event attended by their head of state, her immediate heir and the heir's heir. Yet this wasn't a spectacle of interest only to audiences with tangible links to those present. The marriage of the Prince and the commoner gripped a global audience, reaching places not represented at the ceremony and without historical ties to Britain or, like the U.S., long independent of its Crown. The world loves a love story, and we're thirsty for narratives of hope in difficult times. But more than that, the wedding achieved something exceptionally rare: it united watchers around the world as one.

Some 750 million people watched Prince William's father, the Prince of Wales, marry Lady Diana Spencer in 1981; 2.5 billion were drawn by Diana's 1997 funeral. Many commentators perceived in Diana's death a second death—of the world's unfathomable but undeniable fascination with Britain's monarchy. Then came news of her son's engagement, and the fascination kindled again. Estimates suggest that in addition to the London throngs, upwards of 2 billion people saw the wedding on TV or online, triggering the mysterious alchemy that turns spectators into participants in their own history. As the bride stepped out of the car, you knew that a huge chunk of humanity was watching as you were, straining

Pippa, superstar *Seconds after Philippa Middleton emerged from the Rolls-Royce that carried her to the site of William and Kate's nuptials, social-media sites lit up with praise for the 27-year-old sister of the bride. The maid of honor looked stunning in an ivory gown by Sarah Burton at Alexander McQueen, the same designer who dressed Kate—so much so that many among the multitude around the world watching the wedding on TV thought that Pippa, someone they had barely heard of before the ceremony, had stolen the show from the bride*

for a first glimpse of the dress as you were, caught up in the moment as you were. As William and Kate exchanged their vows in London's historic Westminster Abbey, a significant portion of our fractured, fractious planet, for those moments at least, shared an idea and a dream.

William and Kate were granted the titles Duke and Duchess of Cambridge as their wedding day dawned. And though admiring observers agreed that the new Duchess looked the part, a few doubters remained. In the months since the engagement was announced on Nov. 16, 2010, Britain's finger-wagging tabloids had repeatedly pointed out that Kate's antecedents were not only modest but plebeian, including miners and manual laborers. The newspapers attributed her brief split from William in 2007 to class tensions. They mentioned her mom Carole Middleton's lèse majesté in chewing gum in the presence of the Queen; they openly mocked the family's business, Party Pieces, a mail-order company that retails decorations and other "partywares." Just two years after she first caught their attention, the tabloids had dubbed Prince William's girlfriend "Waity Katie." Her sole ambition, they implied, was to snare the future King. But the royal bride carried off the nuptial day with a poised, radiant serenity that silenced her critics and won her a world of admirers.

Kate's elegant gown, by Sarah Burton of the late British designer Alexander McQueen's studio, was widely hailed, while younger sister Pippa, who bore its long train,

As William and Kate exchanged vows, a significant portion of our fractured, fractious planet ... shared an idea and a dream

SAMIR HUSSEIN—WIREIMAGE—GETTY IMAGES

Hats on steroids. The royal nuptials went to their heads

For Americans, the royal wedding took place just as the sun was rising on a Friday morning. But that didn't dampen the celebration: millions of early-birds gathered to share tea, crumpets and delicious bits of gossip as the events across the Atlantic unfolded. And what was Topic No. 1? Why, the women's hats, of course. Above are only a few of the millinery creations that provoked admiration, wonder, bewilderment—and in a few cases, the pity and terror that Aristotle declared essential to tragedy. Princess Beatrice, second from left in the bottom row, the daughter of Prince Andrew and former wife Sarah Ferguson, was deemed the day's reigning fashion victim.

---

was also a vision in white. Westminster Abbey, which can be gloomy at times, was scrubbed clean and brightened by large, potted hornbeams and maples. The Queen, just turned 85 and in the 59th year of her reign, was even brighter than the abbey, in a buttercup-yellow ensemble. Britons, world champions of pomp and circumstance, once again displayed their mastery of majesty.

Next question: Can the new Duchess of Cambridge do the same? The challenge awaiting the bride is without precedent: to strengthen, not dilute, the Windsor brand by metamorphosing from commoner to royal. Her success will depend in part on whether Britons are prepared to accept that such a transformation is possible. And the extent to which they do will in turn give Kate—and the rest of us—fresh insight into how a once hidebound nation is adapting to an age of ceaseless revolutions. ■

—By Catherine Mayer

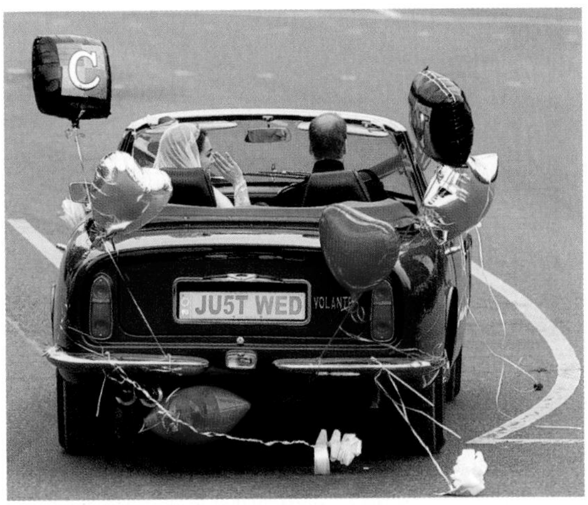

Good sports *After a luncheon at Buckingham Palace, the newlyweds tool off to change for an evening party*

TOP: AFP—GETTY IMAGES; BOTTOM: CHRIS ISON—PA—AP IMAGES

A Nightmare In Norway

A lone terrorist stages a bombing as a diversion, then attacks unarmed youths on a sheltered island

When tragedy strikes, people tend to huddle together. That instinct—the need to gather and console one another in a moment of collective shock and pain—was Anders Behring Breivik's most insidious weapon in the arsenal he carried onto the tiny island of Utoeya, a wooded retreat in Lake Tyrifjord, about an hour's drive from Oslo.

Breivik, a 32-year-old Norwegian with blue eyes and a short crop of blond hair, arrived at the lakeside pier on Friday, July 22, dressed as a police officer. Hours before, a car bomb that he planted and detonated in the heart of the Norwegian government quarter in Oslo had ripped through the neighborhood, killing eight people and injuring many more. Yet the Oslo bomb was a murderous distraction, a meticulously planned bit of misdirection. The apparent attempt on the life of Prime Minister Jens Stoltenberg, at first thought to be the work of Islamist extremists, kept Norway's crack antiterrorism squad busy in Oslo while Breivik drove to Utoeya. He flashed his ID—which was fake but good enough to fool the security guards at the lake. And they waved him past. As Simen Braenden Mortensen, one of the camp guards, told the daily *Verdens Gang,* "It all looks fine, and a boat is called, and it carries him over to Utoeya. A few minutes passed, and then we heard shots," he said.

When he arrived at the island, Breivik found people hurrying into the main house at the retreat. Some were crying, walking arm in arm as they tried to make sense

TOP, LEFT TO RIGHT: MORTEN EDVARSEN—AFP—GETTY IMAGES; CATERS NEWS—ZUMAPRESS.COM; MORTEN HOLM—SCANPIX—AP IMAGES

Day of horror *At far left, campers on the island of Utoeya are removed by police after Breivik's attacks.*

At center is the small island, only 26 acres (10.6 hectares) in size, which rests in a lake some 20 miles (32 km) outside Oslo.

Breivik diverted police with a bombing in downtown Oslo, near left, that killed eight people earlier in the day

of the images of devastation filling TV screens in the aftermath of the Oslo bombing, which by then was being described as Norway's 9/11 moment. The guests on the island had particular reason to be rocked by the events in Oslo's government quarter. Each year, for as long as anyone can remember, the youth wing of the Norwegian Labor Party has gathered there. Founded in 1887, Labor is Norway's largest political party, and it has been the major force in the country since World War II. Gathered at the retreat of the Labor Party's youth wing were the country's future leaders, the teenage children of the ruling élite. By the time Breivik approached the main house, witnesses recall, about 80 people had gravitated there.

Breivik, in his policeman getup and wearing earplugs, urged the people to move into the main house. "I'd like to gather everyone," he said, according to a camper. Then, brandishing an automatic machine gun, he ran into the building and opened fire on the crowd.

Focusing on Oslo, it took more than an hour for Norwegian police to comprehend and respond to the massacre that was unfolding at the idyllic island retreat. Children ran screaming out of the house and across the grounds, only to be gunned down in their tracks. Breivik, according to witnesses, remained calm, methodically seeking out his victims behind stones and bushes, where they attempted to hide. People who live near the island described horrific scenes as scores of teenagers rushed for the water as the shooter fired on them.

By time he was arrested Friday evening, Breivik had killed 69 people on the island of Utoeya in addition to the eight in Oslo. Norwegian police described Breivik as a conservative, right-wing extremist and a Christian fundamentalist who is an adherent of conspiracy theories about Eurabia: the idea that Muslims are infiltrating European society with the goal of dominating it.

In travel guides, Norway is often described as the most beautiful place on the planet, a tiny nation of 4.8 million with an enormous countryside of natural beauty, icy mountains and deep, dark fjords, northern lights and the midnight sun. As they count their losses in the bitter days and months ahead, Norwegians will long for a more innocent past. Utoeya is now a symbol of what has changed, says Prime Minister Stoltenberg: "A paradise island has been transformed into a hell." ■

—*By William Boston*

"Necessary" *Breivik in custody. He freely confessed to his deeds, which he described as "atrocious but necessary." As of Oct. 15, he had not yet been formally charged with committing the mass murders*

RIGHT: JON-ARE BERG-JACOBSEN—AFTENPOSTEN—AP IMAGES

In Brief

New Nations, Old Problems

JUBA, SOUTH SUDAN On July 9, two new nations were born when Africa's largest country split in two: a smaller, mostly Arab and Muslim Sudan ruled from the old capital, Khartoum, and a mainly black African and Christian South Sudan with its capital in Juba. The road to separation was long and bloody: 2 million people died in two civil wars—1955 to 1972 and 1983 to 2005—between Sudan's government and southern rebels. But as TIME's Alex Perry observed, "Rather than heralding peace, the split is creating two weak and unstable countries and yet more conflicts."

South Sudan was born after a Jan. 9 referendum mandated by the 2005 Comprehensive Peace Agreement that ended the second civil war, in which the south voted for secession, with 99% in favor. But even before the split, war broke out between the Islamic regime of President Omar Hassan al-Bashir in Khartoum and the Nuba, ethnic black African rebels of the Nuba Mountains, whose state of South Kordofan ended up inside the new, northern nation. Meanwhile, South Sudan's President, Salva Kiir Mayardit, seemed bent on ruling as an autocrat, bolstered by the riches of his new nation's oil resources.

MEDIA

Tabloid Tempest

"This is the most humble day of my life," Rupert Murdoch declared to a House of Commons committee on July 19, as the mogul's tabloid empire in Britain came under intense fire. Murdoch, 80, the Australian-born founder, chairman and CEO of the world's largest media company, News Corp., was forced to stop publication of his fast, raw and raunchy Sunday paper, *News of the World,* after reports emerged that it had hired a private investigator who allegedly hacked the mobile phone of slain 13-year-old Milly Dowler after her disappearance in 2002.

New charges followed: News Corp. employees and hirelings were alleged to have hacked the phones of the families of dead British soldiers, of the royal family, of celebrities. As the scandal spread, senior police officials resigned, as did PM David Cameron's chief press aide, a former Murdoch employee. The PM's ties to top News Corp. executives were heavily criticized. When Murdoch and son James testified before Parliament, they claimed to be unaware of the extent of the hacking.

New Faces at the Helm

Stephen Harper of Canada's Conservative Party retained his position as PM in a March election, but many nations around the world, including both Thailand and Japan in Asia, continued to see unusually rapid turnover in leaders.

Yingluck Shinawatra, Thailand

The 44-year-old executive won election as the politically fractious country's first female Prime Minister on July 3. The leader of the populist Pheu Thai Party is the younger sister of Thaksin Shinawatra, the polarizing former PM who was toppled in a 2006 military coup.

Stephen Harper, Canada

Harper's Conservative minority government fell in March, triggering a general election. On May 2, the Conservatives added to their numbers in Parliament to become a majority party.

Ollanta Humala, Peru

Humala, 49, a former military man, defeated Keiko Fujimori in a run-off election on June 5, after Humala changed the Gana Peru coalition's leftist positions and moved it toward the center.

Yoshihiko Noda, Japan

Naoto Kan stepped down as PM and leader of the ruling Democratic Party on Aug. 26, damaged by his response to the March 11 tsunami. Noda, 54, won a party election and became PM on Sept. 2.

SUDAN: ROBERTO SCHMIDT—AFP—GETTY IMAGES; MURDOCH: MICHAEL REYNOLDS—EPA; LEADERS, FROM TOP: SAKCHAI LALIT—AP IMAGES; MIKE RIDGEWOOD—GETTY IMAGES; RAUL SIFUENTES—LATIN CONTENT—GETTY IMAGES; SANKEI VIA GETTY IMAGES

Late in the Year, a Russian Spring?

MOSCOW *Angry citizens gathered in Red Square on Dec. 10 to protest parliamentary elections that they charged were rigged, even though the results sharply reduced the size of ruling party United Russia's majority in the Duma. The demonstrations centered on current PM Vladimir Putin of the United Russia party, who plans to run for President in March 2012. Putin, 59, has already served two terms as President and is widely viewed as more powerful than current President Dmitry Medvedev. But the tough former KGB man is increasingly unpopular, and international commentators noted that Russia's state-run media reported the protests accurately.*

A Debt Crisis Staggers the European Union

EUROPE Citizens rioted and governments fell as the massive sovereign debt of poorer nations in the European Union rocked the Continent. Greece was hardest hit: citizens took to the streets to battle police as its government initiated harsh austerity measures in return for emergency aid by large European banks to avoid a default. The crisis toppled the government of PM George Papandreou in November; technocrat Lucas Papademos was chosen to lead a national unity government. Italy's three-time PM Silvio Berlusconi retired the same month and was also replaced by a technocrat, Mario Monti.

On Dec. 9, the E.U. nations, led by German Chancellor Angela Merkel, agreed to a set of reforms that proposed the creation of a European Fiscal Union to unite their economies more closely than ever. Britain's PM, David Cameron, refused to join them, saying it would hand over too much of his nation's sovereignty to E.U. bureaucrats.

Papademos

Monti

Gbagbo Is Toppled In Ivory Coast

ABIDJAN **On April 11, former President Laurent Gbagbo, Ivory Coast's leader since 2000, and his remaining entourage surrendered to rebel forces, above, in the country's de facto capital, Abidjan. It was the conclusion of a five-month-long crisis that saw at least 3,000 people die in horrific brutality. Gbagbo's refusal to concede victory to Alassane Ouattara, the winner of the November 2010 election, triggered the conflict that saw not only a lockdown of the country's economy but also the ravaging of Abidjan. French forces fighting under a U.N. mandate helped end the stalemate and arrest Gbagbo.**

TOP: ANDREY RUDAKOV/BLOOMBERG VIA GETTY IMAGES; BOTTOM, FROM LEFT: LOUISA GOULIAMAKI—AFP—GETTY IMAGES; GEORGES GOBET—AFP—GETTY IMAGES; ISSOUF SANOGO—AFP—GETTY IMAGES

Life

A whirlpool created by the March 11 offshore earthquake swirls off Oarai City, Japan

REUTERS—KYODO—LANDOV

WORLD

Japan's Triple Ordeal

A massive undersea earthquake spawns a deadly tsunami and triggers a nuclear crisis

KOJI HAGA WASN'T JUST CLOSE TO THE HUGE tsunami that devastated northern Japan on March 11, 2011. He was on top of it. Somehow the fishing boat captain kept his pitching vessel upright as the churning force of the wave attacked the shore, turning his coastal community of Akaushi into a graveyard of rubble and leaving some 20,000 people dead or missing in the country's northern prefectures. TIME's Hannah Beech met Haga barely 24 hours after he'd returned to the spot where his house once stood. Aside from the roof, which landed not far from his building's foundations, Beech reported, there was nothing recognizable that remained of his home. A few mementos were scattered in the wreckage: his waterlogged family albums were lodged in the axle of an upturned car, while his daughter's pink stuffed animal lay facedown in the mud.

As Beech watched, Haga ignored most of these keepsakes. His first priority was scooping up sodden rice to take back to his hungry family and neighbors, who had escaped the wave by scrambling to higher ground. Yet even as the fisherman packed the ruined grain into a sack, he displayed the fortitude and generosity that distinguished the people of this devastated region of Japan

JIJI PRESS—AFP—GETTY IMAGES

Overwhelmed *The waves of the tsunami breach the seawall in Miyako in Iwate prefecture, as the elaborate coastal defenses Japan erected against such surges proved inadequate*

Anguish *Yoshikatsu Hiratsuka, 66, weeps after he searched the remains of his house, devastated by the tsunami, and was unable to locate his mother. As many as 20,000 people died in the disaster*

in the wake of the tsunami: Haga was embarrassed that the rice was spoiled, but he invited Beech to take some. The next day, Haga would join Akaushi's other survivors to begin the slow clearing of debris and then the reconstruction of a village virtually wiped off the map. "We'll all try our best to do this together," he said, not a note of pity in his voice. "That's the Japanese way, isn't it?"

Haga and his fellow Japanese were living through the gravest natural disaster in their nation's history, a three-headed monster consisting of a huge undersea earthquake that unleashed a massive tsunami, which in turn led to a nuclear crisis. The nation's ordeal began at 2:46 p.m. on March 11, when a magnitude-9.0 quake—the largest in Japan's recorded history and the planet's fourth largest quake since 1900—occurred in the Japan Trench, a subduction zone off the east coast of the Japanese archipelago.

A subduction zone is where one tectonic plate is moving under another. The March 11 event was a "thrust" earthquake, a variety of a "dip-slip" quake in which the ground is actually thrust upward, causing surface deformation of the seabed. The displacement at the surface caused by this deformation excites a big column of water—a tsunami, Japanese for "great harbor wave."

These killer waves are stealthy: they can travel hundreds or even thousands of miles across the ocean at speeds of up to 600 m.p.h. (966 km.p.h.), almost undetectable as long as they remain submerged in the deep, for they are essentially widespread, massive increases in the volume of water, rather than the curling waves we are used to see breaking upon shorelines. But when the massive swells approach the uphill slopes that link shorelines to the ocean floor, tsunamis compress and speed up, racing up the incline and emerging from the surf as giant walls of water bearing overwhelming power, forces of mass plus energy that can destroy everything in their path.

And that's what happened on March 11 across the coastlines of northeastern Japan. The temblor, centered 18.6 miles (30 km) below the surface, caused a 23-ft. (7 m) tsunami that swept through coastal areas in Fukushima prefecture and a 13-ft. (3.9 m) tsunami in nearby Iwate prefecture. Dramatic aerial images taken over Miyagi prefecture, which is largely flat farmland, showed a dark, debris-filled expanse of water and mud sweeping in from shore and

YOMIURI SHIMBUN—AFP—GETTY IMAGES

Swept away *The power of the tsunami waves left this fishing trawler lying on its side amid the streets of Hachinohe, a city in Aomori prefecture on the northeast coast of Japan*

enveloping everything in its path, from houses to schools, cars and roads. Seldom has nature's dominion over the works of man been more apparent, more widely and closely documented on video—or more heartbreaking.

In the weeks that followed, an anxious world watched Japan struggle to dig out from its natural tragedy even as it fought a tragedy abetted by man, as workers strained to control damaged reactors at the nuclear power plant in Fukushima, where leaking radioactive steam forced nearby residents to evacuate. By September, the toll from the earthquake and tsunami was tallied at as many as 20,000 dead, while tens of thousands of people remained homeless. The government estimated the tsunami's damage at $300 billion, which would place it among the most expensive natural disasters on record.

"We'll all try our to best to do this together. That's the Japanese way, isn't it?"

—KOJI HAGA, FISHING BOAT CAPTAIN

Perched on the Ring of Fire, an arc of seismic activity that encircles the Pacific Basin, Japan is one of the most earthquake-prone countries in the world, and it has long been regarded as one of the best equipped to handle one. Having survived the great Tokyo quake of 1923, which killed at least 100,000 people; the utter devastation of World War II; and, in 1995, an earthquake in Kobe that took more than 6,400 lives, the country has done more than most when it comes to disaster preparedness.

Every year since 1960, Japan has observed Disaster Prevention Day on Sept. 1, the anniversary of the 1923 quake. The nation also boasts the world's most sophisticated earthquake early-warning systems, and it has consistently upgraded its building codes to save lives during earthquakes. During the March 11 quake, the skyscrapers of Tokyo, about 231 miles (373 km) from the epicenter, were badly rattled, swaying to and fro. But the buildings stood, a tribute to the nation's foresight.

Japan also boasts a tsunami warning service, set up in 1952, that consists of 300 sensors around the archipelago, including 80 aquatic sensors that monitor seismic activity 24/7. The network is designed to predict the height, speed, location and arrival time of any tsunami heading for the nation's coast. On Japan's east coast, where tsunamis frequently hit, hundreds of earthquake and tsunami-proof shelters have been built. Some cities have built tsunami walls and floodgates, so that the waves don't travel inland through river systems. But as videos showed in horrifying detail, the seawalls and floodgates weren't built to withstand the power of tsunamis as mighty as the March 11 monster: the waves swept all before them.

In the days following the disaster, TIME's Beech reported from Japan, authorities' inability to respond spontaneously and creatively to uncharted events prevented aid from getting to survivors quickly enough. Even four days after the quake, highways were mostly devoid of the kind of aid convoys that usually converge on a disaster zone, in part because of the colossal scale of the catastrophe and central-government weakness.

Of equal importance was the early cone of silence around the damaged Fukushima nuclear power plant. Even as overheated fuel rods caused radiation to leak in what scientists called the worst nuclear accident since Chernobyl, information from the government and power-plant officials was piecemeal and tardy.Yet as the country waited anxiously to see what would happen at the crippled reactor site, ordinary Japanese quietly came to one another's rescue. For volunteer aide worker Kenichi Numata, there was little time to even explain his actions, much less process his own sorrow. After the earthquake, he told Beech, he and 1,600 others dashed to the airport in Sendai, the region's largest city, and watched as dozens perished in the surrounding tide of mud and debris. Numata knew that his house was among those that had been swept away by the tidal wave. But he had a self-imposed task: organizing dazed locals who were trying to figure out whether their missing family members might be alive. Just in the past few hours, he had told several people their kin had died. It was not an easy job. "I'm sorry," he said, bowing deeply in apology to Beech. "But I had better go back to work." ■

PAULA BRONSTEIN—GETTY IMAGES

After the onslaught *Rescue and recovery workers, faces masked for protection against disease, carry the body of a tsunami victim in Kesennuma in Miyagi prefecture, which was hit hard in the disaster*

DIGITALGLOBE VIA GETTY IMAGES

Nuclear Nightmares. Thousands are forced to leave their homes when the tsunami cripples a power plant

The tsunami that struck northern Japan on March 11, 2011, not only devastated coastal towns but also spawned a nuclear crisis, as waves crashed into six reactors at the Fukushima Daiichi nuclear power plant, above, shutting down power lines that fed systems that cooled the reactors. The breakdown bred grave fears of a nuclear meltdown and the possible release of radioactive matter. As a waiting world watched in the days after the tsunami—and as Japan's government and plant operator the Tokyo Electric Power Company kept a tight lid on information about the crisis—no meltdown occurred, but there was no question that radioactive matter was leaking from the plant, workers were still struggling to cool down the reactors, and the outcome was far from certain.

Fears soared after authorities extended the evacuation zone around the plant, established early in the crisis, from 12 to 18 miles (20 to 30 km). Unsafe radiation levels were found in tap water as far away as Tokyo, 136 miles (220 km) south of the Fukushima plants. Milk and leafy vegetables from Fukushima were banned both nationally and abroad. As time passed without a full meltdown, the crisis eased. But the government was widely criticized for withholding information about the plant: it was not until late July that officials revealed that a memo issued in April stated that some 1,600 plant workers had been exposed to dangerously high levels of radiation during the crisis.

By late summer, authorities said that radioactive emissions from the site had dropped to a fraction of what they were in early days of the accident, and attention shifted to a secondary disaster: the contamination of the region around the plant, and the plight of the thousands of people who were driven from their homes.

On Aug. 22 Tokyo reported that higher than expected levels of radioactive contamination might keep areas near the plant off-limits for human habitation for years, or even decades. Said Chief Cabinet Secretary Yukio Edano: "There are areas near the nuclear power plant where the level of radiation is very high and it cannot be denied that there may be areas where it will be difficult for the residents to return for a long time. I am very sorry for that."

The 90,000 residents who live within a 12.4-mile (20 km) radius of the stricken reactors—nearly all of whom had been homeless for more than five months—were likely to be a lot sorrier. Government data showed that some areas within the evacuation zone were contaminated with radiation levels 25 times higher than Tokyo's safety limit for annual exposure. Even if the ongoing leakage of radiation from the plant can be stopped, those levels mean that thousands of homes may remain too contaminated to live in for years or decades, as the case has been with the exclusion zone that now surrounds the Chernobyl plant in Ukraine.

Only days after the Aug. 22 announcement, the reverberations from the nuclear crisis helped bring down the government of Japan's Prime Minister, Naoto Kan, after only 15 months in office. The tsunami, it seemed, had claimed one more victim.

DISASTERS

Torn Asunder

The deadliest U.S. tornado in decades devastates a Missouri town

Wasteland *In the twilight hours after the storm passed, shortly before 6 p.m., Joplin residents survey the half-mile-wide swath of ruin the tornado carved out amid the city streets*

NICCOLO UBALDUCCI—POLARIS

WARM AIR RISES. THE EARTH IS AN ELEGANT MACHINE, and this is one of its simple and tireless engines, recycling the oceans into life-giving rains, wafting rainbow-striped hot-air balloons into clear skies, putting the dance in the flame of a birthday candle. This law must not be thwarted. There is hell to pay.

On Sunday, May 22, sometime after 5 p.m. in the Midwest, a column of warm air struggled against a ceiling of colder air pouring in from the north. When at last the irresistible engine pushed a hole through the ceiling, the pent-up energy shot upward in a mad rush, whirling and roaring. It could have happened anywhere on the mostly empty prairie. This time it happened as the air mass passed through the south side of Joplin, Mo.

It sucked the roof from St. John's Regional Medical Center and shattered the windows, sweeping reams of medical records heavenward. It snipped utility lines like thread and pulverized St. Mary's Church and school yet left the giant cross towering over the rubble, unscathed. Chewing through homes, apartment houses and storefronts, the vortex crossed Main Street and climbed

Amid the ruins *President Obama, Missouri Governor Jay Nixon, on left, and other officials visited families a week after the twister roared through Joplin. At right, a child is carried to safety after the storm passed on May 22*

a hill toward the house where Kay Boyd, 63, was listening to KSN meteorologist Caitlin McArdle's increasingly urgent command: "Take cover! I'm telling you, take cover right now!" Boyd wanted to hide in the tub, but her husband Ed, 65, steered her into a closet beneath the stairs. "It seemed like it went on forever," she said—the broken glass and plaster and beams hammering at the closet door in the screaming wind—but forever was only a matter of seconds.

Aggie Elbert, 84, cowered in her basement with her daughter and small grandchildren, thankful for a cache of hard hats as her house exploded overhead. The storm crested the hill and started down toward Joplin High School, splintering a neighborhood as it went. Pamela Merriman, just shy of 28, forgot the taco meat on the stove, called for her children, rushed them into the bathroom and wrapped them in a quilt. In the deafening wind, she hugged Seth, 9, and Samia, 3, on the floor of the shower, scarcely able to hear the old brick fireplace tumbling through the living-room floor, or the garage door crashing through the wall beside her, or the bleachers from the high school ball field as they whistled across a city block and wrapped around her front-yard tree.

The tempest bent the goalposts flat to the ground and riddled the gridiron with timber, pipe fragments, bits of asphalt shingles and a bouquet of artificial flowers. It peeled open the high school gym, flinging a roof girder hundreds of yards across Iowa Street. Another school, Franklin Tech, fell in a heap.

With the recklessness of youth, Allen Godby, 22, raced toward his mother-in-law's house with a carload of assorted family members. He is from Oklahoma, "so I've been outrunning tornadoes all my life," he says. He did not outrun this one. Pulling into the yard, he tore at his daughter's seat belt as the twister finished with the high school and crossed the street. Godby fell to the ground on top of 4-year-old DaNia. Spinning debris raked his back and head. He felt himself being sucked from the ground and dug his fingers into the mud. When at last he looked up, he thought the whole family must be dead—but one by one they called weakly from the rubble.

Onward the great storm churned, destroying some 2,000 structures, damaging 6,000 more, tearing up 1,800 acres of city built over many decades. It ripped its way across Range Line Road, a busy commercial corridor, burst the Home Depot, dropped the Walmart roof onto the heads of shoppers. Jonathan Merriman's cell phone rang. It was his wife Pamela calling. She was trapped with the kids in the shower under the garage door. She needed him, and he wanted to go to her, but first he had to survive. He crawled under the sinks in the Walmart bathroom as the roof flew off and the walls fell in—and the sinks somehow held steady and Jonathan was safe.

After the storm passed, so was Pamela Merriman. Two days following her escape, she looked into the tiny triangle of space that had held her and her two children after the roof dropped and the walls tumbled and the bathroom was shoved into the living room under the garage door. Imagine a doghouse, then go a little smaller. "I feel really good that I was able to protect my children,"

FROM LEFT: POLARIS; MIKE GULLETT—AP IMAGES

Good neighbors *At left, Alisha Kelly, of nearby Neosho, Mo., offers food and bottled water three days after the storm. "We are just individuals who want to help," she said. At right, an impromptu sign bears good news*

she said. She surveyed her former possessions, the stuff of a world now lost. "I'd be happy with just walking away from all of this," she concluded. "Dump it all and just start over. Happy birthday—I'm alive."

The Joplin monster was the deadliest tornado in the 61 years that the National Weather Service has been keeping official statistics: by late September, the death toll stood at 162. At its most furious, the half-mile-wide killer maxed out on the Enhanced Fujita scale at EF-5, its spinning winds roaring in excess of 200 m.p.h.

No one in Joplin—a growing community in southwestern Missouri where the Show Me State meets up with Oklahoma and Kansas—expected such a storm, though perhaps people should have. Joplin is smack in the middle of Tornado Alley, where the tornadoes were frequent and furious throughout the late spring. Just weeks earlier, a squadron of twisters, some EF-5, tore through Tuscaloosa, Ala., on a rampage through the South. Is this the "climate chaos" that scientists of global warming have been warning about? At the opposite end of Missouri from Joplin, miles of prime farmland were soaked under the record floodwaters overflowing the Mississippi and its tributaries. Pattern or coincidence?

The answer awaits more data. The heat-trapping effect of greenhouse gases is well proved; the precise impacts on local climates are less clear. Whirlwinds and floods have been with us forever—old hat even in the days of the Bible scribes. But as humankind multiplies and spreads, more and more people risk encountering extreme and deadly weather. In 2011, tornadoes killed more than 500 Americans and destroyed billions of dollars' worth of property. Perhaps the surprise is that the toll was not even higher. The population of the U.S. has more than doubled since 1950 and sprawled. Thousands of square miles have been populated in the tornado zone in the suburbs and exurbs of cities like Dallas, Kansas City and Nashville. We can cover the land and alter the atmosphere, but we can't change the rules of nature. Warm air rises. ■

—David Von Drehle

$1 BILLION

The amount of funds paid out by insurance companies to cover damage as of mid-September. Further payouts were expected to total an additional $1 billion to $2 billion

1,800

The number of acres in the middle of the city that were devastated by the twister; many homes and buildings nearby were unaffected

162

The death toll from the storm as of mid-September. Some 5,000 people were left homeless by the tornado

FROM LEFT: JULIE DENESHA—GETTY IMAGES; KENNETH M. RUGGIANO—REDUX

CATHY ZURAW—THE CONNECTICUT POST—AP IMAGES

NATURE

Climate Chaos Extreme weather stalks the U.S. Is there a pattern?

Welcome to the new normal: In 2011, the U.S. suffered through one of its most extreme weather years in recent history. In Texas, drought parched the grasslands, and wildfires ran wild. Tornadoes, once confined to a narrow swath of land in the Midwest, hammered Tuscaloosa, Ala., and other Southern cities, while the monster EF5 twister that devastated Joplin, Mo., was the deadliest single tornado to strike the U.S. in six decades. Northern cities that dispatched aid to New Orleans after Hurricane Katrina smashed into the Crescent City in 2005 found themselves bracing for disaster themselves, after Hurricane Irene made landfall in North Carolina and roared its way up the nation's East Coast.

Nor was the nation's year of extreme weather confined to the summer months. After all the hot-weather excitement, it was easy to forget that the year began with a monster storm, dubbed the Groundhog Day Blizzard, that crouched over most of the nation early in February, dumping enough snow to bring activity in cities from Boston to El Paso and many points in between screeching to a halt. So much snow fell in the West over the winter that spring melting caused heavy flooding along the Missouri and Mississippi rivers.

For years, scientists have been warning that the globe's gradual warming trend will likely unleash an age of "climate chaos," in which the weather will get more extreme and less predictable. It's too soon to tell if it is here, climatologists say, but the evidence is mounting. ■

TOP: HANS PENNINK—AP IMAGES; BOTTOM, FROM LEFT: LARRY W. SMITH—EPA; RON T. ENNIS—ZUMA PRESS—CORBIS

A Hurricane in New England

A seafront home in Fairfield, Conn., left, collapsed under the pressure of the storm surge driven by Hurricane Irene, which coursed up the East Coast after making landfall on Aug. 27 on North Carolina's Outer Banks. As the storm headed straight for the nation's largest urban corridor, breathless TV, radio and Internet coverage followed its every move. Fortunately, the storm weakened as it traveled, ending up as a tropical storm by the time it hit New York City, where authorities had shut down the city's mass transit system and evacuated tens of thousands from low-lying locales.

Though many Americans enjoyed a laugh at the oversaturated coverage of a storm that undersaturated some places, Irene caused major damage in many areas, including upstate New York and Vermont, where river flooding reached heights unseen for centuries, and some communities were entirely cut off from the outside world for days. During its passage across the Caribbean and into the U.S., the storm killed more than 50 people and caused more than $10 billion in damages.

Flooding in the Northeast

When Hurricane Irene failed to create a Hollywood-style crisis along the East Coast, the nation's media looked elsewhere for excitement. Yet only a week after Irene passed through, two smaller systems, Tropical Storm Lee and Hurricane Katia, dumped rain from Louisiana to New York State and Pennsylvania, where the Susquehanna River Valley was hard hit. Above, a minivan is stranded in Binghamton, N.Y., on Sept. 9. More than 100,000 people were evacuated from their homes along the path of the storms.

Drought and Wildfires in Texas

The fires at night were big and bright, deep in the heart of Texas, as residents of the Lone Star State endured the dryest 12 months (August 2010 to July 2011) in recorded history. Drought is not unusual in the nation's Southwest, but the 2011 edition set records, thanks to a strong La Niña effect, originating in the Pacific Ocean, which shut off the pipeline of moisture to the U.S. South; the dry weather followed, as if someone had simply turned off the tap. The arid conditions in turn fed wildfires that roared across the state, wreaking havoc: From the beginning of the fire season, which authorities date as Nov. 15, 2010, through late September, 2011, more than 23,500 fires had burned up more than 3 million acres and destroyed more than 2,700 homes, right, and as many as 4,000 other structures.

Lab Report

Alternatives to Nitpicking

HYGIENE Since the common head louse, *Pediculus humanus capitis,* developed resistance to the formerly effective shampoos Rid and Nix, parents have been looking for new ways to keep kids from becoming, well, lousy. Now two new treatments have emerged to give high-priced hand nitpicking, offered in salons, some competition.

The LouseBuster is a contraption that dries up lice in 30 minutes by blowing warm air at the hair's roots, where the lice tend to hang out; it gets rid of 99.2% of shampoo-resistant nits, according to an independent study. Coming soon: bacteria-based Natroba, a solution that has worked nearly twice as well as Nix in clinical trials. Its $36 price tag undercuts the LouseBuster, though its kill rate is a bit less, at 86.7%.

SPORT

Concussion: Heads Up!

The number of U.S. kids who experience brain concussion is rising rapidly, and the growth of athletics for girls is adding to the increase. High school football players alone sustain 100,000 full-blown, diagnosed concussions per year. As awareness of the injury's dangers also rises, lawmakers are imposing new rules governing how kids should be assessed for concussions and when they should be eligible to play, while equipment manufacturers are being pushed to redesign their product lines and reform the testing standards that allow the industry to police itself.

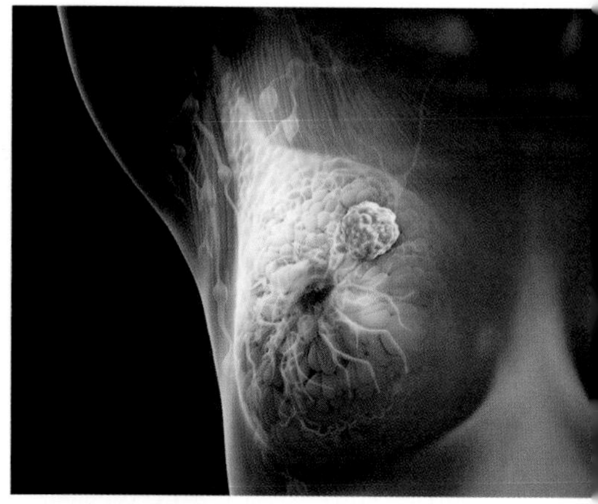

Mapping Breast Cancer

GENETICS In April, researchers at the Washington University School of Medicine announced they had sequenced for the first time the entire DNA code of one type of breast-cancer tumor. The genetic maps provided some intriguing clues: the tumors studied harbored more than 1,700 genetic mutations, most of which were unique to the women in whom they originated. Of the few gene mutations shared by many of the women, some were previously associated with cancer in other studies, and some were new. The sheer number of genetic abnormalities suggests that cancer may vary from one person to the next, but most of the changes actually fed into common pathways of tumor growth. These processes could become targets of broadly useful new drugs, opening an era when doctors may be able to match each patient to the best possible treatment.

Cell Phones and Cancer: The Debate Goes On

CANCER The Federal Communications Commission, the National Cancer Institute and countless other bodies have agreed that cell phones are safe to use. But charges that cell phones can cause brain and other cancers remain a hot topic. In 2011, two new studies further clouded the issue. On May, 31 scientists from the International Agency for Research on Cancer classified cell-phone-radiation exposure as "possibly carcinogenic to humans." Within weeks, a different study of more than 2.8 million Danish adults found that those who had used a cell phone for 11 to 15 years were no more likely than new users or nonusers to develop acoustic neuromas, slow-growing, non-cancerous cells, near their ears. It's frustrating, but a definitive answer on cell-phone safety remains on hold for now.

CLOCKWISE FROM TOP LEFT: SCIENCE PICTURE CO—SCIENCE FACTION—GETTY IMAGES; JOE PATRONITE—GETTY IMAGES; SCIENCE PICTURE CO—SCIENCE FACTION—GETTY IMAGES; MARK EDWARD ATKINSON—GETTY IMAGES

Breakfast of Champions: Coffee, Eggs and Chocolate

NUTRITION *"Want to get healthy?" Dr. Mehmet Oz inquired of* TIME *readers in August. "Then forget about diet soda and low-fat foods. Instead, tuck into some eggs, whole milk, salt, fat, nuts, wine, chocolate and coffee." Despite conventional wisdom, Oz argued, all of these foods and many more can be beneficial to your body; it's overindulging in them that brings health problems. According to Oz, "The simple rules that divide things into good-food and bad-food categories tell you only a small part of a complex story."*

Doctors: Vaccinate or Leave

PREVENTION When the *British Medical Journal* announced in January 2011 that the seminal 1998 study linking vaccines to autism was an "elaborate fraud," parents who had refused to have their kids vaccinated were expected to flock back to their doctors' offices—not that they ever should have stayed away. But nonsense has a way of sticking around, and vaccination rates in the U.S. have continued to flag. Now, to prevent the spread of disease, some pediatricians are telling parents, in effect, Vaccinate your kids or find another doctor.

NUMBERS

28
BILLION

Estimated amount of dollars Americans spent on dietary supplements in 2010, according to the Nutrition Business Journal

0

Number of times since 1994 that the U.S. Food and Drug Administration has approved the safety or efficacy of such supplements

A Genetic Link for Depression

DEPRESSION Confirming findings from 2003, University of Michigan researchers reported early in 2011 that a particular gene may increase the risk of depression, but only in combination with an added, nongenetic factor: a stressful life event. People with one form of a protein that ferries serotonin, a mood-related neurotransmitter, are especially prone to depression when faced with traumatic events, such as being diagnosed with a medical illness or being a victim of childhood abuse, they found.

TOP: JAMES WORRELL; BOTTOM, FROM LEFT: SCIENCE PHOTO LIBRARY—GETTY IMAGES; NIKOLAY TITOV—GETTY IMAGES

Cubs *Chua poses with daughters Lulu, left, and Sophia*

LEFT: MARTIN SCHOELLER FOR TIME—AUGUST, STYLING BY STEFANIE SYATT/BERNSTEIN & ANDRIULLI; RIGHT: BRENT HUMPHREYS FOR TIME

PROFILE

Amy Chua

The "Tiger Mom" has answers for raising kids of all stripes

FOR MANY READERS, IT WAS THE "LITTLE White Donkey" incident that pushed them over the edge. That's the name of the piano tune that Amy Chua, 48, Yale law professor and self-described "Tiger Mother," forced her 7-year-old daughter Lulu to practice for hours on end—"right through dinner into the night," with no breaks for water or even the bathroom, until at last Lulu learned to play the piece. For other readers, it was Chua calling her older daughter Sophia "garbage" after the girl behaved disrespectfully—the same thing Chua had been called as a child by her strict Chinese father. Chua's kids, Sophia and Louisa (Lulu), were never allowed to have playdates, watch TV or get anything less than A's in school. They played instruments of their mother's choosing (piano, violin) and practiced for hours under close watch.

When *Battle Hymn of the Tiger Mother,* Chua's proudly politically incorrect account of raising her children "the Chinese way," arrived in bookstores on Jan. 11, 2011, her parenting methods became the indignant talk of every playground, supermarket and coffee shop. Small wonder the first thing Chua wants you to know is that she is not a heartless monster. "Everything I do as a mother builds on a foundation of love and compassion," she told TIME. Love and compassion, plus punishingly high expectations: in short, the Chinese method of parenting.

Most surprising of all to Chua's detractors may be the fact that many elements of her approach are supported by research in psychology and cognitive science: for example, her assertion that American parents go too far in insulating their children from discomfort and distress. Another pet peeve: Americans' habit of "slathering praise on their kids for the lowest of tasks." Westerners often laud their children as "talented" or "gifted," she says, while Asian parents highlight the importance of hard work: her approach, she argues, pays higher dividends in the long run. Love her or hate her, Chua made Americans finally regard their child-rearing practices with fresh eyes: a "Sputnik moment," courtesy of a fired-up mom. ■

—By Annie Murphy Paul

PROFILE

Rob Bell

A preacher questions the afterlife, and finds there's hell to pay

AS PART OF A SERIES ON PEACEMAKING, IN late 2007, Pastor Rob Bell's Mars Hill Bible Church put on an art exhibit about the search for peace in a broken world. It was just the kind of avant-garde project that had helped power Mars Hill's growth (the Michigan church attracts 7,000 people each Sunday) as a nontraditional congregation that emphasizes discussion rather than dogmatic teaching. The show included a quotation from Mohandas Gandhi, and a visitor to the exhibit had stuck a note next to the Gandhi quotation: "Reality check: He's in hell."

Bell was struck. Really? he recalls thinking. Gandhi's in hell? Somebody knows this? Without a doubt? And that somebody decided to take on the responsibility of letting the rest of us know? So begins Bell's controversial 2011 best seller, *Love Wins: A Book About Heaven, Hell, and the Fate of Every Person Who Ever Lived.*

The standard Christian view of salvation is the acknowledgment that Jesus is the Son of God, who, in the words of the ancient creed, "for our salvation came down from heaven ... and was made man." In the Evangelical ethos, one either accepts this and goes to heaven or rejects it and goes to hell. Bell, a tall, 40-year-old son of a Michigan federal judge, begs to differ. He suggests that the redemptive work of Jesus may be universal—meaning that, as his book's subtitle puts it, "every person who ever lived" could have a place in heaven, whatever that may be.

Such a simple premise, but Bell's slim, lively book ignited a new holy war in Christian circles. When word of *Love Wins* reached the Internet, one Evangelical pastor, John Piper, tweeted, "Farewell Rob Bell," attempting to evict Bell from the Evangelical community. In North Carolina, a young pastor was fired by his church for endorsing the book.

Bell's work sheds light on a shift within U.S. Christianity. More indie rock than "Rock of Ages," his style of doctrine and worship is playing a larger role in religious life, and the ferocity of the reaction to it suggests that his views are emerging as a force to be reckoned with. ■

—By Jon Meacham

In Brief

Casey Anthony: Not Guilty

ORLANDO Ending a murder trial that captivated many Americans, a Florida jury on July 5 found Casey Anthony, 25, not guilty in the alleged 2008 murder of her 2-year-old daughter Caylee, whose duct-taped corpse was found after a six-month search. The sheer horror of the act—and the notion that her mother committed it—catapulted the case from local live-at-5 sideshow to tabloid sensation, especially after pictures of Anthony partying enthusiastically even while her daughter was missing appeared on the Net.

Anthony had already been convicted by loud voices in the media—so the verdict came as a shock to many. But as TIME's John Cloud pointed out, "Casey Anthony is guilty of many things. She is an enthusiastic liar. She was an indifferent mother ... Even after her daughter went missing, Anthony partied and got a tattoo. But the state of Florida did not make a good case that Anthony murdered her daughter. In acquitting Anthony, the jury made the right call." Anthony, who was freed shortly after the verdict, was ordered to pay some of the expenses incurred by authorities in the search for Caylee.

NUMBERS

63 MILLION

The amount, in dollars, Russia will charge, starting in 2014, for a round-trip flight on a Soyuz spacecraft to the International Space Station, now that the U.S. shuttle program has concluded

---

0

The number of Eastern cougars remaining alive in the U.S. The U.S. Fish and Wildlife Service officially declared the animal extinct in 2011

Signs of Water on Mars

PASADENA, CALIF. In a paper published in August in the journal *Science*, planetary scientists announced that new images beamed back by the Mars Reconnaissance Orbiter (MRO), which has been circling the Red Planet since 2006, had produced the first compelling evidence that there is flowing, salty water on the Martian surface.

In recent years scientists have found increasing evidence that Mars was once very wet. Mineral deposits, ancient shorelines, dried-up lake beds and long-empty waterways all attest to the sloshingly aquatic place the planet once was. Most of the water was lost to space owing to Mars' low gravity and tenuous atmosphere, scientists suspect. Any that was left contracted into ice coverings in polar latitudes or perhaps retreated into the soil. If anything warm and liquid existed deeper underground, there seemed no way to find it. The MRO images changed that, showing the appearance of seasonal streaks at key points on the Martian surface, looking like the tracks of water rivulets running downslope, collecting at the base of the incline and then evaporating back into the atmosphere. The evidence appears as brownish streaks at the bottom of the image below, taken during the Martian summer.

FROM LEFT: JOE BURBANK—AP IMAGES; NASA/JPL-CALTECH/U. OF ARIZONA

A Popular Pope Is Beatified, but His Church Remains Under Fire

ROME *Pope Benedict XVI prays before the coffin of popular Pontiff John Paul II on May 1, when the current Pope beatified his predecessor, the first major milestone toward sainthood. Thousands of pilgrims flocked to Rome for the celebration. But 2011 was another rocky year for the Roman Catholic Church, as the long-running scandals involving sexual abuse of young people by clergy continued to undermine the church's authority. In a riveting speech to Parliament in July, Ireland's PM, Enda Kelly, denounced what he called "the dysfunction, disconnection, élitism–and the narcissism–that dominate the culture of the Vatican to this day."*

TOP: ALBERTO PIZZOLI—AFP—GETTY IMAGES. BOTTOM, FROM LEFT: NASA VIA AP; MICHAEL OKONIEWSKI/BLOOMBERG VIA GETTY IMAGES; POLARIS

Farewell to the Shuttle Era

CAPE CANAVERAL, FLA. An estimated 1 million people from across the U.S. crowded the Florida coast on July 8 to watch the final liftoff in the U.S. space shuttle program. The *Atlantis* crew—commander Chris Ferguson, pilot Doug Hurley and mission specialists Sandra Magnus and Rex Walheim—spent 12 days in orbit, docking with the International Space Station to provide supplies and equipment. The 135th shuttle mission took place 30 years after the first craft lifted off; the program was marred by two deadly disasters, in 1986 and 2003.

To Frack or Not to Frack?

WASHINGTON Many questions surround the practice of shale gas drilling, especially the controversial hydraulic fracturing methods, a.k.a. fracking, energy firms use to get the gas found in shale. An August report by an independent panel convened by the Department of Energy largely endorsed the use of shale gas for its economic and potential environmental benefits but called for much more oversight of the practice in the future.

End of a Legal Ordeal

PERUGIA, ITALY Overturning a controversial December 2009 conviction, an Italian appeals court on Oct. 3 found American Amanda Knox, 24, and former boyfriend Raffaele Sollecito, 27, not guilty of complicity in the murder of British student Meredith Kercher, 21, in 2007.

In a case that made global headlines, Knox had been branded, her family charged, as a "sex-crazed she-devil" by Italian authorities and media before a court convicted her and Sollecito of aiding small-time drug runner Rudy Guede in the bloody knife slaying of Kercher. Knox, who had spent most of the previous four years in prison, was released and immediately returned to Seattle with her family.

Sport

Daredevils ride high at the Day of Giants surfboat race in Auckland, N.Z., on Feb. 2

PHIL WALTER—GETTY IMAGES

DILIP VISHWANAT—GETTY IMAGES

An October Classic

The St. Louis Cardinals come from behind—again and again—to beat the Texas Rangers in the World Series

On Oct. 28, when David Murphy of the Texas Rangers took the final swing of a memorable, sometimes magical, World Series, Allen Craig, the St. Louis left fielder, forgot his fundamentals as the ball sailed toward him. "Honestly, when he hit it I turned the wrong way," said Craig while standing on the Busch Stadium field after Game 7, the championship confetti spread across the grass. "And then I had to look over my shoulder and try to pick it up again, and it was bouncing left and right in the air. I was like, 'Just catch it, please,' " Craig recalled, "so we can go home with the victory. It's crazy."

Crazy, yes, as the St. Louis Cardinals became the World Series champions for an 11th time, for the ball found the middle of Craig's glove, sealing the Cards' convincing 6-2 victory over the Rangers in the deciding game of a Series

The Rangers would get their title, for surely St. Louis could not come back again, right?

that will be recalled for decades. During the last month of the regular season, and throughout an excellent postseason, the Cardinals would just never go away. After making a series of moves to shore up its bullpen around the trade deadline, the team struggled, falling 10½ games back in the wild-card race in late August to the Atlanta Braves. Around this time, baseball commissioner Bud Selig even met up with Cardinals manager Tony La Russa and gave him a "Get 'em next year" pep talk.

Not to worry, Bud: the Cardinals got back into the race, and won a game on the last day of the regular season to sneak into the playoffs. They came back from a 2-1 game deficit to beat the heavily favored Philadelphia Phillies in the first round, and then took six games to bounce the confident Milwaukee Brewers (the team with the best home record in all of baseball) out of the National League Championship Series. The Series that followed, against a fine Rangers squad, was a nail-biter that featured a record-book slugging show by the Cards' Albert Pujols in Game 3 and a nutty bullpen-telephone foul-up that made the widely respected La Russa look foolish in Game 5.

But it was Game 6 that baseball fans will never forget. In the top of the seventh, with the score tied 4-4, Adrián Beltré and Nelson Cruz slugged back-to-back solo home runs that put the Rangers just nine outs away from the title. These guys would be kings of Texas! The Rangers entered the bottom of the ninth with a 7-5 lead and ace closer Neftalí Feliz on the mound. With runners on first and second and two outs, the St. Louis season came down to third baseman David Freese, 28, a hometown hero who grew up in a local suburb dreaming of playing for the Cardinals. Freese hit a 1-2 fastball the opposite way, into deep right field, where Cruz looked as if he had a read on it: the Series felt finished. But Cruz mistimed his run to the wall and couldn't catch up to the ball. Both runs scored on the Freese triple, and the Cards were saved one more time.

But before the crowd came down from its high, Josh Hamilton sent it reeling again. With a man on first in the top of the 10th, Hamilton slugged the first pitch from reliever Jason Motte over the right-field wall. Now, it was 9-7 Rangers. They'd get their title, for surely St. Louis could not come back again, right? Wrong. In the bottom of the 10th, the Cardinals cut the lead to 9-8. With two outs and outfielder Jon Jay on third, Lance Berkman had two strikes on him—before he tied it up again, incredibly, with a single to right-center field. Bedlam at Busch!

Champs *At top, St. Louis first baseman Albert Pujols, 31, celebrates his third home run in Game 3, a feat that tied him with Babe Ruth and Reggie Jackson as the only players to hit three homers in a Series game; Pujols became a free agent after the Series. Below, David Freese is all smiles as fans cheer after the Cardinals won the Series. On the left page, the Cards celebrate their improbable win*

TOP: EZRA SHAW—GETTY IMAGES; BOTTOM: DILIP VISHWANAT—GETTY IMAGES

After the Rangers failed to score in the top half of the 11th, Freese led off the bottom half for St. Louis—and lofted a shot off that landed in a patch of grass beyond the center-field fence. The Cardinals had won 10-9, in a game that was widely hailed as one of the greatest ever played.

The deciding 7th game was an anticlimax, as the Cards cruised to their 6-2 win over the Rangers. On the Monday after the Series ended, La Russa, 67, declared he would retire after 33 years as a manager and three World Series championships. Perhaps he knew he could never top a Series that was both crazy—and an instant classic. ■

Legend *Prior to the shocking events of 2011, Paterno was one of the icons of coaching, respected not only for his winning ways but also for refusing to coddle his athletes and insisting that they study hard and earn their diplomas*

JUSTIN K. ALLER—GETTY IMAGES

SPORT

Penn State's Fall from Grace

A beloved college football coach neglects his obligations, and his university pays the price

THE PENN STATE UNIVERSITY FOOTBALL team's motto is "Success with Honor," and no coach seemed to live up to that credo more than Joe Paterno, the Nittany Lion leader for more than 45 years. Paterno, known simply as "JoePa" in a vale in central Pennsylvania called Happy Valley, won 409 games in his career—a Division 1 record—and two national championships. His players usually graduate, no small feat in major college athletics, so often merely a training camp for the NFL. "Coaches have the same obligations as all teachers," Paterno, 84, wrote in *Paterno: By the Book,* his 1989 autobiography. "Except that we may have more moral and life-shaping influence over our players than anyone else outside of their families."

Moral influence: no one seemed to wield it better than Paterno. But the events of late 2011 suggested that both the revered coach and other authorities at the university had fumbled their ethical obligations. Because of his failure to report a child sex abuse case directly to authorities, Paterno lost his job and his reputation as a role model. On Nov. 9, the university's board of trustees fired Paterno and university president Graham Spanier. Earlier that day, Paterno released a statement in which he called the situation "one of the great sorrows of my life. With the benefit of hindsight, I wish I had done more."

Penn State's woes began on Nov. 5, when the Pennsylvania attorney general's office charged Jerry Sandusky, 67, a defensive coach at Penn State for 33 years who retired after the 1999 season, with 40 counts related to the sexual abuse of eight minors. In addition, two Penn State administrators—athletic director Tim Curley and senior vice president for finance and business Gary Schultz—faced criminal charges for allegedly lying about their knowledge of Sandusky's behavior, and failing to report it to authorities, as required by Pennsylvania law. (Sandusky, Curley, and Schultz all denied the charges.)

The most severe allegation, according to grand jury testimony, involved a graduate assistant, later identified as current Penn State wide-receivers coach Mike McQueary, who claimed he saw Sandusky raping a 10-year-old boy in the showers of the Penn State football facility in 2002. Paterno testified that McQueary told him about the nature of the incident but left out the graphic details. By informing Curley, his superior, about the episode, Paterno met his legal obligation. But what about his moral obligation? Football coaches at big state-run institutions have more clout than many governors. Paterno, the biggest man on campus, chose to punt this problem to a PSU bureaucrat.

On the night of Nov. 9, thousands of Penn State students, furious over Paterno's dismissal, rioted in the town of State College, turning over a local TV satellite van in a modern-day version of shooting the messenger. The incident seemed to confirm widespread accusations that at Penn State, veneration for a football program outweighed concerns for the alleged victims of sexual abuse: success had trumped honor. Two nights later, seeking to reverse that impression, thousands of students, alums and locals convened outside the university's Old Main building and held a candlelight vigil in honor of all victims of abuse. One of the organizers read a letter from an anonymous female student who detailed her own sexual abuse—and thoughts of suicide—as many in the crowd wept.

On Saturday, Nov. 12, Penn State's shaken team faced Nebraska. Before the contest, players walked rather than ran onto the field; they met at its center and knelt in prayer, as many in the crowd of 107,903 fans joined them. Nebraska won, another sign that it might be a long time before Happy Valley was happy again. ■

Accused *Former Penn State coach Jerry Sandusky, 67, is at the center of the allegations of sexual abuse*

Aftermath *On the night Paterno was dismissed, some students rioted in downtown State College, Penn., turning over a TV news van, left. Two nights later a much larger group marched in honor of the victims of the alleged abuse*

TOP: ANDY COLWELL—THE PATRIOT NEWS—AP IMAGES; BOTTOM, FROM LEFT: MICHAEL HENNINGER—POST GAZETTE—AP IMAGES; PATRICK SMITH—GETTY IMAGES

PATRICK MCDERMOTT—GETTY IMAGES

PROFILE

Novak Djokovic

The Serb was superb in 2011, winning three of four Grand Slam titles

WHEN HE WON THE U.S. OPEN TENNIS championship on Sept. 12, Novak Djokovic kept himself under control, even as his delirious entourage bounced in their seats. The reigning cut-up of the court didn't eat some strange substance, as he did at Wimbledon, where he chomped on grass after winning the tournament (though he did give the hard court surface a little peck). He didn't dance to hip-hop music or pull out one of his impersonations, or act goofy for the crowd, which he's fond of doing.

No, Djokovic, 24, just slouched in his chair, taking it all in. Turns out that tearing up men's tennis can be exhausting. "I feel drained," the Serbian player said after beating Spain's Rafael Nadal, 6-2, 6-4, 6-7, 6-1, in the final. In his gracious on-court speech after the match, Nadal turned to face Djokovic and said "What you've done this year will probably never be repeated."

What Djokovic had done this year was to win the Australian Open, Wimbledon and the U.S. Open, three of tennis' four Grand Slam tourneys. Nadal, the master of the clay court game, won the French Open, after the third of the sport's current top trio, Roger Federer, managed to oust Djokovic in Paris.

In the U.S. Open final, after Djokovic won the first and second sets, Nadal staged a third-set charge that electrified the New York City crowd. It's not that the fans disliked Djokovic; they just wanted to see more tennis. Djokovic lost the third-set tiebreaker, held his serve in the first game of the fourth set, then called for a medical timeout; his ribs, legs and back were hurting. He took a painkiller, and then put a hurt on Nadal, winning the next six games, and the match.

After his triumph in New York City, Djokovic's record stood at 64-2 in 2011—a .970 winning percentage. What's his secret? Some say it was his decision to stop eating gluten when he learned he was allergic to the protein. After the match, he was asked what he had eaten the night before. "Last night, I didn't have any gluten," the new champ replied, "and tonight, I will have a bunch of gluten—and alcohol." ■

PROFILE

Rory McIlroy

Tiger who? Golf's newest superstar is a charming 22-year-old

AMERICA'S GOLF FANS HAVE BEEN RESTLESS OF late, struggling to stay interested in the sport after Tiger Woods' downfall, thirsting for someone fresh to keep them hooked. And sport doesn't get much fresher than Rory McIlroy, the young golf phenom from Northern Ireland, who shot a 2-under-par 69 in the final round of the U.S. Open at the Congressional Country Club in Bethesda, Md., on June 19, giving him a preposterous 16-under-par score for the tournament and an eight-shot victory. It was McIlroy's first major championship, and the crowd at Congressional utterly adored the curly-haired, Guinness-loving chap with the big smile. McIlroy filled their needs, his non-American roots no hindrance to their approval.

Such is the power of a transcendent performance. In winning, McIlroy broke a slew of records. He reached double-digits under par faster than any golfer in U.S. Open history, doing it in 26 holes. He had the lowest U.S. Open score after 36 holes (131), 54 holes (199) and 72 holes (268). In 2000, Woods had tied the prior record for lowest under-par score at a U.S. Open, when he shot a 12-under at Pebble Beach. Tiger at Pebble—that was the performance to which all U.S. Open efforts would be measured. Thanks to his 16-under-par score, you will now have to match McIlroy.

While McIlroy's golf mechanics were extraordinary, his mental gymnastics are the lasting achievement of his win. If the world didn't weep for McIlroy after the 2011 Masters in April, it certainly felt for him. The youngster entered the last day of play with a four-shot lead, and looked as if he would cruise to the green jacket. But then he triple-bogeyed the 10th hole, bogeyed the 11th, double-bogeyed the 12th and hit his tee-shot on 13th into the creek. Ouch! He shot an 80, and finished tied for 15th. During the round, the boyish McIlroy looked on the verge of tears. But when Charl Schwartzel won the tournament, McIlroy showed off his mental chops. The next day, he posted a picture on Twitter; he and Schwartzel were smiling on a plane headed for their next tournament. "Flying to Malaysia with charl!" McIlroy wrote. "Glad one of us has a green jacket on!!"

McIlroy couldn't duplicate his Open magic in the final two Grand Slam events, finishing in midfield at the British Open and PGA championships. But even the phenoms can't win them all—and McIlory has time, lots of time, on his side. ■

ROBERT BECK—SPORTS ILLUSTRATED

Tour de France

After years when cycling's greatest event seemed to be more about drug tests than road-racing, the 2011 Tour was blessedly free of doping allegations. In an exciting finish, Australia's gifted, diminutive racer Cadel Evans, 34, surged into first place in a time trial on the Tour's next-to-last day and became the first athlete from Down Under to win the Tour.

SPORT

Champions. Sports fans welcome a fresh new crop of superstars

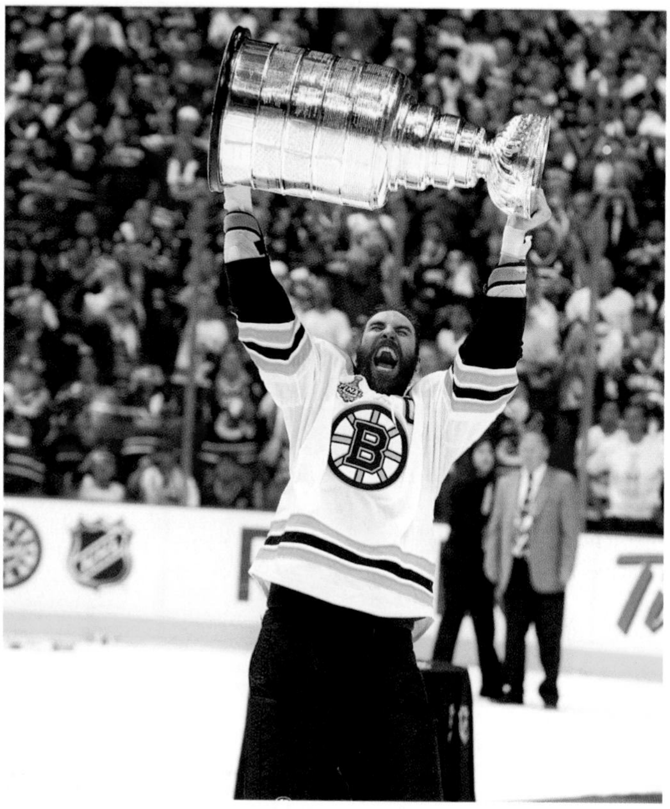

The Stanley Cup

Oh, Canada. For a nation that lives for hockey, what could hurt more than to have the Boston Bruins' Zdeno Chara, left, getting intimate with the Stanley Cup, the legendary trophy of the National Hockey League? To rub salt in the wound, Boston won the title on Canadian soil, defeating the Vancouver Canucks 4-0 on June 15 in the seventh game of the championship series. The insult to national pride was so severe that fans leaving the arena started a mini-riot.

The NBA Championship

Germany's Dirk Nowitzki, right, and his Dallas Mavericks schooled the Miami Heat, 105-95 on June 12, in the sixth and deciding game of the NBA championship series, as Heat stars LeBron James and Dwyane Wade played poorly. Nowitzki, 33, a 13-year veteran who had never won an NBA title, was named the MVP of the finals.

The NBA's entire 2011-12 season was in peril after the players' contracts ran out in the fall, owners locked them out and new talks failed. After 16 games were missed, the two sides reached a deal on Nov. 26 under which teams will play a 66-game season beginning Dec. 25.

RIGHT: ANDREW D. BERNSTEIN—NBAE VIA GETTY IMAGES; LEFT, FROM TOP: PASCAL PAVANI—AFP—GETTY IMAGES; DAVID E. KLUTHO—SPORTS ILLUSTRATED

DALLAS
41
DALLAS
11
DALLAS
31
HEAT
6
Budweiser

On Court, in with the New

After years in which the hierarchy of the tennis world was as rigid as the pecking order at Versailles, the ancient regime began to crumble in 2011. The big news came on the men's side, where Serbia's Novak Djokovic, 24, found an extra gear in his game; he won Wimbledon and the Australian and U.S. opens. The master of the clay court, Spain's Rafael Nadal, 25, (in blue), won the French Open. Once the man to beat, Roger Federer, 30, won no majors in 2011, though he was responsible for ousting Djokovic in Paris.

On the women's side, the long dominance of the Sisters Williams began to falter. Comeback queen Kim Clijsters, 28, won the Australian Open, while China's Li Na, 29, won the French Open, the first Asian woman to do so. A Czech, Petra Kvitova, 21, far left, beat Russia's Maria Sharapova, 24, to win Wimbledon's coveted silver salver.

Though Serena Williams, 30, looked strong in reaching the finals of the U.S. Open, she lost the match to the steady Aussie Samantha Stosur, 27, at top, after Williams had a meltdown and argued with a judge, as she had in 2009. Big sister Venus Williams, 31, had a challenging year and withdrew from the U.S. Open due to a recently diagnosed autoimmune disease.

TOP, CLOCKWISE FROM TOP LEFT: MIKE STOBE—GETTY IMAGES FOR USTA; CLIVE BRUNSKILL—GETTY IMAGES; PAUL WEBB—REX FEATURES VIA AP IMAGES. BOTTOM, FROM LEFT: ANDREW REDINGTON—GETTY IMAGES; DOUG MILLS—THE NEW YORK TIMES—REDUX; CHARLES KNIGHT—REX FEATURES VIA AP IMAGES; STUART FRANKLIN—GETTY IMAGES

Golf's Majors: Four Championships, Four New Champions

After the long Reign of Tiger ended, golf fans were wondering who would take the place of the sport's dominant player. But if 2011 is any guide, the answer may be: no one, fortunately. Far from a one-man show, the year's Grand Slam events turned into a fine clutch of tournaments, each with its own stamp.

The year's major tourneys began with little-known South African Charl Schwartzel, 27, left, winning the Masters Tournament in Georgia. Northern Ireland's Rory McIlroy, only 22, dominated the U.S. Open in Maryland, and his countryman Darren Clarke, 43, won the famed Claret Jug of Britain's Open Championship. The PGA Championship, the year's last major, featured a riveting playoff between Keegan Bradley, 25, in red at right, and Jason Dufner, 34, in pink. Bradley won, with a thrilling last-minute comeback.

Packers: A League of Their Own?

In a memorable Feb. 6 Super Bowl XLV that came down to the final drive, the Green Bay Packers beat the Pittsburgh Steelers, 31-25 to win a high-scoring duel between old-school NFL franchises. The Packers raced out to a 21-10 halftime lead, but Steelers quarterback Ben Roethlisberger, 28, started to sizzle in the second half. Green Bay quarterback Aaron Rodgers, 27, fired right back, threading several clutch passes that brought the Vince Lombardi Trophy home to Titletown.

But Rodgers and his green-and-gold legions were just getting started, it seemed; after the summer break, they continued to dominate every team they faced. The Pack went undefeated well into the 2011 season, and Cheeseheads were dreaming of a new dynasty.

A Soccer Upset in Germany

A strong U.S. team seemed likely to win the 2011 FIFA Women's World Cup soccer tournament in Germany, as they faced a smaller but plucky Japanese squad in the final match in Frankfurt on July 17. The Americans had proved their mettle with a sensational victory over Brazil in a quarterfinal match, when a left-footed cross from Megan Rapinoe, 26, flew past Brazil's flailing goalkeeper and was met by a perfect header at the back post from veteran Abby Wambach, 31, for the tying goal—in the last minute of injury time in the last overtime period. Then, behind the inspired goalkeeping of Hope Solo, 29, the U.S. prevailed in the penalty shoot-out, 5-3.

The Americans next cruised over France in the semifinals, 3-1, on the way to what seemed a certain title—to everyone except the Japanese. Though the U.S. dominated the ball and was clearly the more talented team, the players blew too many scoring chances—they outshot Japan, 27-14—and let the nonplussed Japanese hang in there to win the match on penalty kicks after a 2-2 deadlock. At right, Wambach, in white, is boxed out near Japan's goal in the final.

TOP: DOUG PENSINGER—GETTY IMAGES. BOTTOM: LARS BARON—FIFA VIA GETTY IMAGES

The Culture

Miami's New World Symphony rehearses for the Jan. 30 opening
of its new auditorium, designed by Frank Gehry

CLAUDIA URIBE—COURTESY NEW WORLD SYMPHONY

Wicked Webs

After a long, sticky run-up, *Spider-Man* takes the stage

AT LEAST FOUR PERFORMERS WERE INJURED doing the show's technically demanding aerial stunts. Opening night had to be delayed repeatedly as the production was being worked on. The critics slammed it even before it was finished. Finally, most ignominiously, director Julie Taymor, celebrated for her marvelous design and direction of *The Lion King* for Disney, was ousted, and a new creative team was brought in to make major revisions in the Broadway musical that had become a late-night TV punch line.

When *Spider-Man: Turn Off the Dark* opened officially on June 14, after the longest and most troubled preview period in Broadway history, the show itself seemed almost an anticlimax. The red-carpet crush was so chaotic (among the celebs in attendance: Steve Martin, Matt Damon, Barbara Walters and former President Bill Clinton) that the opening curtain had to be delayed—naturally—by 45 minutes.

When the actors finally took their bows, nearly three hours later, the drama still wasn't over. During the curtain calls, Bono and the Edge, the U2 members who helped launch the show, wrote the score and then got caught in a quagmire, acknowledged the standing ovation and thanked everyone for their patience. Then Bono introduced "the person without whom none of this would be possible"—Taymor, still credited as the show's "original director," who graciously took her bows alongside the people who got her canned.

Oh, and as for the musical in between all the theatrics? It's not that bad. In truth, *Spider-Man* was never quite the disaster that the early reviews a little too gleefully suggested. The chief problem was the murky and overly ambitious script by Taymor and Glen Berger, who felt the need to embellish a generic superhero saga with all sorts of mythological mumbo-jumbo. In a limited sense, the salvage job (overseen by Philip William McKinley) is successful. Nearly all of Taymor's narrative experiments were junked; the story is simpler and more logical; there are more love scenes—and more dull stretches. Meanwhile, the set design is as strikingly inventive as ever; the Bono-Edge score really rocks; there's more humor; and an upbeat new number provides a lift at the start of Act II. And there's still plenty of flashy aerial acrobatics. *Spider-Man* 2.0 is better than the original, but sadly, it's still just a cut above an ordinary Broadway spectacle. ■

—By Richard Zoglin

All's well that ends well *Original director Julie Taymor joins Bono and the Edge of U2 after the opening-night performance of* Spider-Man: Turn Off the Dark. *Above, principals Reeve Carney and Jennifer Damiano*

WALTER MCBRIDE—CORBIS (2)

Oh What a Beautiful Mormon

The creators of *South Park* turn their satiric gaze on religion

ON PAPER, IT SEEMED LIKE AN EPIC MISmatch: Trey Parker and Matt Stone, the bad boys behind *South Park,* TV's most notoriously potty-mouthed cartoon show, bringing their irreverent act to Broadway, the family-friendly environs of *Wicked* and *Jersey Boys.* But think again: their musical, *The Book of Mormon,* became the year's biggest hit. After all, in recent years, Broadway has been trying to attract younger, hipper audiences, with shows like *Avenue Q,* 2004's profane puppet musical, whose co-creator Robert Lopez was Parker and Stone's collaborator on the new show. Broadway now opens its doors to rap musicals and drug-fueled punk-rock extravaganzas like 2010's Green Day–powered *American Idiot.* How freewheeling is Broadway getting? The year also brought the straight drama *The Motherfu--er with the Hat.* A few years ago, there would have at least been more hyphens.

For all their renegade street cred, Stone and Parker are closet lovers of the classic Broadway musical. Parker, 41, grew up in a small Colorado town watching Rodgers and Hammerstein revivals by the local community theater, the Evergreen Players. He went on to star in high school musicals, majored in music at the University of Colorado and transferred his musical-theater passion to his college friend Stone (a math major, two years younger), taking him to see *Miss Saigon* in London. The pair's 1999 feature film, *South Park: Bigger, Longer and Uncut,* was a cheerily old-fashioned (if foulmouthed) musical that nabbed an Oscar nomination for Best Song.

Indeed, *The Book of Mormon* turned out to be less incendiary than an average episode of *South Park.* It focuses on a team of fresh-faced Mormon missionaries who are sent to Uganda to try to convert a band of villagers beset by poverty and pestilence. Though the show makes mild fun of the wackier elements of the Mormon creation story—prophet Joseph Smith's discovery of holy golden tablets in upstate New York—it steers clear of more hot-button issues associated with the religion, like polygamy. Critics cheered, Tony Awards voters swooned—and the Salt Lake *Tribune* quoted Anne Christensen, a 22-year-old Mormon New Yorker, as saying, "I was expecting to be offended but was pleasantly surprised by how incredibly sweet it was." ■

—RZ

JOAN MARCUS—BONEAU/BRYAN-BROWN VIA AP

The odd trio
A pair of young Mormon missionaries encounter a witch doctor in Uganda in The Book of Mormon, *which won nine Tony Awards*

School's Out

The good sports of Hogwarts thrash Voldemort, as a long-running book-and-film series winds up

FOR THE MILLIONS OF KIDS WHO GREW UP reading the books and seeing the movies—and for the rest of us, thrown into an imaginary and enthralling adolescence—the wizarding world of Harry Potter was an alternate educational universe. We could play hooky from the cares of our lives by matriculating at Hogwarts School as the permanent pals of the Boy Who Lived. He grew from childhood to early maturity playing Quidditch (ah, the innocence of those first years!), cramming for the Charms finals and preparing to confront the Dark Lord Voldemort, that most powerful creature, whose mission was to kill Harry. All that time, we were at the lad's side, in a reader's or movie watcher's invisibility cloak, hoping Harry knew he could rely on the loyalty of his very dearest friends: Ron, Hermione and us.

A fantasy epic with the unusual goal in these facetious movie days of being iconic, not ironic, the *Harry Potter* films had the benefit of a bedrock constituency: all the fans of J.K. Rowling's wizardly septology. The filmmakers could have filled their Gringotts vaults with cash (some $6.4 billion at the global box office, plus untold quillions in home video) and still failed the source material. Instead, producer David Heyman and his team saw their roles as trustees of a sacred text and their mission to guide Rowling's teen hero to the screen with a buoyant reverence. Planned as the longest single narrative (more than 18 hours) in mainstream-movie history, and with a total production budget of well over $1 billion, the series

fulfilled its gargantuan ambitions. It also proved that children could sit through a 2½-hour movie without a bathroom break. Who knew that cinematic rapture could overcome bladder imperatives?

Harry's tale extends across seven winters, but for us it took a decade: the books were issued from 1997 to 2007, their film versions from 2001 to 2011. The three lead actors have spent half their lives inside their characters. We've seen Daniel Radcliffe (Harry) sprout chest hair and Emma Watson (Hermione) cleavage. The series matured too, finding its true, confident tone with the third chapter, *The Prisoner of Azkaban,* directed by Alfonso Cuarón.

In 2011, it all ended—finally. Harry's senior year took two years; in an act of movie mitosis, Rowling's final volume, *Harry Potter and the Deathly Hallows,* was split into two features consuming more than 4½ hours. Yet the decision by Heyman (who produced all the films), Steve Kloves (who scripted all but one) and David Yates (who directed the last four of the eight) to cut the final book into two features—whatever its sense as a business strategy—meant slowing the story down just as it should rev up. Instead of scooting like a Golden Snitch during a Quidditch championship, *DH1* was struck with a long spell of aimlessness, and the viewer with the curse of ennui. Released in November 2010, the film could have been called *The Dawdling Hallows:* it stranded the kids in the woods for endless scenes of teen moping and marked a steep slump from the high standard the series had set.

Snake-face *Ralph Fiennes as Voldemort in the final film of the series, one of a host of British stars in the eight movies*

With *Deathly Hallows 2,* screenwriter Kloves and director Yates were back on firm footing—hurtling through Rowling's last 300 pages toward the big face-off between Harry and You Know Who (Ralph Fiennes in majestic, maleficent snake-face). Essentially a war movie, *DH2* portrayed the siege of Hogwarts as a children's crusade with late-blooming heroes. (Neville Longbottom, we hardly knew ye.) And it summoned most of its huge, sublime supporting cast for brief appearances—a reminder that the series is a luscious, perhaps unparalleled showcase for this generation's most enduring British actors, as Michael Gambon as Dumbledore and Alan Rickman as Severus Snape took one last curtain call. The audience responded: the film enjoyed a mammoth opening weekend, both in the U.S. and around the world, and quickly became one of the biggest Hollywood hits of recent years.

Now the vast sets have been dismantled, the cast and crew dispersed with final hugs and tearful thanks. We may have ended our journey, but the films will dwell like a house elf in our hearts and on that perpetual-memory machine, the DVD. School's out, boys and girls, but we'll always have Hogwarts.

—By Richard Corliss

All grown up *When Daniel Radcliffe (Harry), Rupert Grint (Ron) and Emma Watson (Hermione) assumed their roles in 2001, left, they were children. At the premiere of the final film in 2011, they had blossomed into young adults—and stars*

The Geek Squad. The battle for digital dominance continues

JEFF BEZOS

Amazon Kindles a Tablet War

On Sept. 28, Amazon CEO Jeff Bezos, 47, stood before a Manhattan audience, Steve Jobs–style, to announce his company's newest digital reader, the Kindle Fire. With a glossy 7-in. color touchscreen and a dual-core processor, the Fire resembles a tablet computer more than an e-reader, although it lacks a camera and a microphone for video calls, popular features on many tablets, and can send and receive data only over Wi-Fi, not cellular networks. But it boasted one strong advantage over competitors: a $199 price tag, far less than the Apple iPad's lowest price, $499, and well under Barnes & Noble's popular Nook Color e-reader, at $249.

Analysts dubbed the Fire an "iPad killer." Yet as TIME's Jerry Brito pointed out, "It's a killer alright, but the victim is not who you think it is: it's cable TV." Bezos' ambitious goal: to link Fire owners to Amazon's online warehouse of more than 18 million e-books, songs, movies and TV shows. For Amazon, content is still king, and the Kindle Fire is the path to its store.

PETER VESTERBACKA

Tycoon of Fowl Play

It was the Year of the Bird for the world's gaming enthusiasts: the crazily addictive Angry Birds crushed the mobile-gaming market with 40 million active users playing monthly and more than 75 million downloads. Now, with the ingenious Peter Vesterbacka, 42, a onetime Hewlett-Packard exec, as head of business development, the game's Finnish maker, Rovio Mobile Ltd., is prepared to besiege the gaming industry's castle.

Thanks to those hostile flying critters, Rovio raised $42 million in a single investment round in 2011. But the company remains offbeat: some senior staff members are given official bird titles. "Mighty Eagle," of course, would be Vesterbacka.

MARK ZUCKERBERG

Facebook Gets a Face-lift

A billionaire and TIME's Person of the Year 2010, Facebook founder Mark Zuckerberg has lots of reasons to smile. He seemed especially ebullient in his keynote address at the company's f8 conference in September, where he announced two major innovations in the world's largest social network (800 million users and counting).

Facebook replaced its Profile—the page each user gets that displays his or her status updates, likes, photos, etc.—with a radically revised version called Timeline, which makes it a cinch to backtrack through a member's entire Facebook history, not just recent activities.

The other big update, Open Graph, lets third-party companies connect their apps and services to Facebook far more seamlessly than in the past—after receiving onetime, blanket permission to do so. Many users howled—but what would Facebook be without a little turmoil?

FROM LEFT: SPENCER PLATT—GETTY IMAGES; FRANK MAY—EPA; DAVID PAUL MORRIS—BLOOMBERG VIA GETTY IMAGES

REED HASTINGS

Divide, Yes—Conquer, No

Reed Hastings was a Marine and a Peace Corps worker before he became an entrepreneur. After misplacing a rental videocassette and racking up a big late fee, he realized his gym had a much better business model than his video-rental store: pay $30 to $40 a month and exercise as little or as much as you want. Netflix revolutionized entertainment distribution by using one of the oldest methods of delivery, the U.S. mail. Now it distributes everywhere —TV, computer, iPad or game console, leading its industry.

In 2010, Hastings, in a roll-the-dice move, shifted the focus of his company from DVD delivery to streaming videos. It worked: by 2011 Netflix had more than 20 million subscribers, up from just over 9 million in 2008. But the company took a nosedive in the summer of '11. First, it sharply raised the price of its streaming and mail order bundle. As users fled in droves, the stock plunged. Then, admitting it had erred, the company unbundled its plan: the streaming service would keep the Netflix title; the mail-order service would separate to become Qwikster. The subscriber bleeding only continued, and the Qwikster scheme was soon dumped, in what critics called one of the greatest strategic blunders in recent business history.

JUSTIN TIMBERLAKE

Now MySpace Is HisSpace

It appears that being a major mover in show biz wasn't enough. Seeking new worlds to conquer, Justin Timberlake made a surprise debut as a a Net guru on June 29, when it was announced he would become an investor in the struggling social media network MySpace, as it was purchased from owner News Corp. for $35 million by a little-known California-based advertising network, Specific Media.

J.T., 30, promised he will be more than a front man for the site. Stay tuned.

CHARLES CHAO

Leading China Online

In 2009 China's government blocked Twitter and shuttered almost all its domestic equivalents. Amid those obstacles, Charles Chao saw an opportunity. A journalist turned accountant who heads Sina, China's largest Internet portal, he turned the company's microblog service into a national site, with the regime's approval.

The result, Sina Weibo, is a high-powered service that Chao, 45, calls a mashup of Twitter and Facebook; wildly popular in China, it had reached 100 million users by the end of February 2011. The site is censored by the regime, Chao acknowledges, but even so, it is one of the freest online platforms in China.

ARIANNA HUFFINGTON

America Online Teams Up with The *Huffington Post*

"This moment will be for *HuffPost* like stepping off a fast-moving train and onto a supersonic jet," said *Huffington Post* co-founder Arianna Huffington, 61, after she announced on Feb. 6 that she was selling her popular, liberal-leaning online news and analysis site to America Online for $315 million in cash and stock. It's a jet that Huffington will have a significant role in piloting. As president and editor in chief of the new, all-encompassing Huffington Post Media Group, she'll also be in charge of AOL's wide-ranging content. As for AOL, this is its biggest acquisition since its ill-fated merger with Time Warner (TIME's parent company) ended in 2009. Once a leading Internet provider, AOL has struggled to define its mission in a rapidly changing online universe.

CLOCKWISE FROM TOP LEFT: FELIPE CAICEDO—GETTY IMAGES FOR NETFLIX; JAMIE MCCARTHY—WIREIMAGE—GETTY IMAGES; NELSON CHING—BLOOMBERG VIA GETTY IMAGES; GUY CALAF—BLOOMBERG VIA GETTY IMAGES

PROFILE

Grant Achatz

His molecular gastronomy leaves foodies foaming at the mouth

TALK ABOUT GREAT EXPECTATIONS: WRITING in TIME, Martha Camarillo called Chicago chef Grant Achatz "the country's greatest 21st century chef." In the 2011 TIME 100 issue, the chef behind the French Laundry and Per Se, Thomas Keller, wrote: "Grant's distinct, thoughtful restaurants refine the standards of our profession through his visionary take on modernist cuisine." In his memoir, *Life, On the Line,* published in the spring of 2011, Achatz (and business partner Nick Kokonas) told his story: his love affair with food; his apprenticeships with Keller and others; and the 2005 opening of his restaurant, Alinea, where he first won fame for his experiments in molecular gastronomy, the shape-shifting culinary magic that transforms familiar dishes into foams, smokes and ice cubes. Most memorably, Achatz, 37, recounted his diagnosis of tongue cancer and eventual recovery.

So: What's for dessert? Achatz and his colleague Kokonas weren't interested in simply duplicating Alinea in other cities, even if it had earned three Michelin stars in 2010; something grander and more daring was in order. Their solution was Next, a restaurant that opened in Chicago in April 2011 with an ambitious agenda: the entire concept and menu of the place would change every three months.

First up: a trip into the Wayback Machine, as Next's menu visited Paris circa 1906, and Achatz cooked up new variations on the legendary cuisine of Auguste Escoffier. Declared TIME's Joel Stein, admittedly an amateur food critic: "[It] tasted both classic ... and totally weird." After three-months, Achatz left the City of Light behind and Next began offering a Tour of Thailand, which Achatz described as presenting "highly manipulated" versions of pad thai and panang curry. You don't have to visit to guess how that menu tastes: both classic and totally weird. ■

MARTHA CAMARILLO—CONTOUR BY GETTY IMAGES

PROFILE

Kristen Wiig

She's shy and unassuming, but there's a madwoman in the attic

THE OFFBEAT COMIC KRISTEN WIIG DIDN'T do any performing at all until she was in her late 20s. Not college theater, not high school talent shows, not little skits for her parents. In fact, she doesn't really like to speak to crowds. "At parties, I'll start talking and notice everyone is looking at me and feel dumb and say, 'Forget it,' and then start eating things," she says.

Which is how she is in movies—no crazy hair, no crazy eyes, no crazy jumping into other actors' shots. After she was in minor roles in two Judd Apatow–produced films, *Knocked Up* and *Walk Hard: The Dewey Cox Story,* Apatow asked her to write a movie that she could star in for his company. So she and Annie Mumolo, a fellow comic, co-wrote *Bridesmaids,* a dude comedy with a chick-flick plot that became a smash hit in the summer of 2011 and was hailed as pioneering a female sensibility in a previously boys-only format. "Although wrapped in slapstick and sweetened with romance," observed TIME critic Mary Pons, "*Bridesmaids* is at its core a shrewd examination of female insecurity."

Wiig, 38, is shy, cool and pretty—not the petri dish of self-doubts from which most comedians are made. At the University of Arizona, she studied art. Then she moved to L.A. and did arty jobs: florist, graphic artist for a plastic surgeon (she illustrated what patients would look like after an operation), decorative painter. When Wiig eases up around people, friends say, her weird creativity comes out, and she does a lot of voices and imitations—so many that the decorative painter she worked with recommended that she see a show by the Groundlings, the L.A. troupe that trained Phil Hartman, Conan O'Brien and Lisa Kudrow.

She zipped through the Groundlings' classes and won tons of stage time performing absurd characters, including a chatty Target salesclerk. By 2005 she was on *Saturday Night Live* doing the Target Lady nearly every week. In fact, there are weeks when it feels as though Wiig is in every *SNL* sketch. The precision of idiosyncratic looks and gestures is what allows Wiig to take one-note characters (a woman who can't keep a secret! A woman who one-ups everyone else's story!) and make them compelling in their quirkiness.

As for Kristen Wiig's opinion of Kristen Wiig: She is not amused. As she told TIME's Joel Stein, "I went through my high school yearbook recently, [and] I was surprised people wrote I had a good sense of humor. I don't remember being funny."

Maybe not. But we will. ■

MICHAEL TRAN—FILMMAGIC—GETTY IMAGES

In Brief

TELEVISION

A New King in the Realms of Fantasy

With the debut of a lavish new HBO series, *Game of Thrones,* above, based on the fantasy series *A Song of Ice and Fire* by George R.R. Martin, 63, the writer's work found millions of new fans. When the long-awaited fifth novel in the series, *A Dance with Dragons,* was published on July 12, it sold 289,000 copies in various formats on its first day of sale. TIME TV critic James Poniewozick declared the HBO series "an epic win ... ambitious and visually stunning ... the most immersive grownup adventure TV has produced since *Lost.*"

TELEVISION

Reality TV for Grownups

A double-barreled dose of long-form documentaries hit TV screens in October. At PBS, resident historian Ken Burns turned (or panned) his attention to a 5½-hour exploration of America's failed experiment in moderation, *Prohibition.*

On HBO, Martin Scorsese, who has documented the career of Bob Dylan and filmed concerts by the Rolling Stones and the Band, profiled an artist from the 1960s, another zesty period fueled by illicit substances. His 3½-hour study, *George Harrison: Living in the Material World,* used new interviews and rare film clips to depict the late Harrison as a unique spirit rather than simply the "quiet Beatle."

MUSIC

Britannia's Adele Rules the Waves

For pop-music fans, nothing beats a summer when a single song dominates the airwaves, appealing to old and young, hipster and square. Such a song was *Rolling in the Deep,* the chuggingly soulful ballad by Britain's Adele Adkins, 21, who performs under her first name. The anti-Gaga, Adele relies on her songwriting and potent pipes to make a splash; her video for *Rolling in the Deep* featured her simply sitting in a chair and singing her heart out. Adele's album *21* topped charts worldwide, but throat problems forced her to cancel U.S. dates in the fall.

CLOCKWISE FROM TOP: HELEN SLOAN—HBO; GEORGE HARRISON: LIVING IN THE MATERIAL WORLD. PHOTO©APPLE CORPS LTD—COURTESY OF HBO; ACTION PRESS—ZUMAPRESS.COM

At the Metropolitan Museum, Long Live McQueen

FASHION *The dark and dramatic creations of fashion designer Alexander McQueen, who committed suicide at 40 in 2010, were celebrated in a major exhibition, "Alexander McQueen: Savage Beauty," at New York City's Metropolitan Museum of Art. Featuring some 100 ensembles and 70 accessories by McQueen, the show was a massive hit with the public: Met officials held it over, extended viewing hours and sold 20,000 new museum memberships during its run. In all, some 660,000 people attended the exhibit.*

THEATER

Get Thee to an Armory

Proving that, if all the world's not exactly a stage, some of its least expected places can serve as one, the Royal Shakespeare Company trekked to New York City in the summer of 2011 and camped out in the cavernous main Drill Hall of the Park Avenue Armory in Manhattan, into which the troupe shoehorned an exact replica of its 930-seat home theater in Stratford-Upon-Avon. In six weeks, 44 actors staged 45 performances of five plays: *Julius Caesar* (above), *King Lear, Romeo and Juliet, As You Like It* and *The Winter's Tale.*

BOOKS

A Final Accounting

When novelist David Foster Wallace committed suicide in 2008 at 46, the author widely admired for *Infinite Jest* (1996) left behind an unfinished manuscript. *The Pale King* was published on April 15, after being hammered into final shape (at 580 pages) by Wallace's friend and editor, Michael Pietsch. Its unlikely subject: the lives of Internal Revenue Service accountants. Praising the work, TIME's Lev Grossman noted that it boasted all of the novelist's customary brilliance yet also "has an emotionally raw quality that Wallace's other novels lack."

TOP: PAUL ZIMMERMAN—GETTY IMAGES (3); BOTTOM LEFT: STEPHANIE BERGER—LINCOLN CENTER; RIGHT: SUZY ALLMAN—THE NEW YORK TIMES—REDUX; BOOK JACKET: NO CREDIT

Milestones

Steve Jobs rolls out Apple's first Macintosh computer, 1984

DIANA WALKER—CONTOUR BY GETTY IMAGES

DIANA WALKER—CONTOUR BY GETTY IMAGES

Steve Jobs

Intense and ingenious, he peered into the future and put it in our hands

STEVE JOBS REMADE THE WORLD WE LIVE IN, but he had no business doing so. He wasn't qualified. He wasn't a computer scientist. He had no training as a hardware engineer or an industrial designer. His expertise was less in computers than it was in the humans who used them. He became the most celebrated, successful business executive of his generation, and he did it all the wrong way. He didn't listen to his customers: It wasn't their job, he explained, to know what they wanted. He will be remembered as a great man, but not necessarily as a kind or good one. His ferocity toward his employees is the stuff of legend: outside Apple, his products urged us to "think different," but inside, there was only one way to think, and that was like Steve.

Maybe Jobs thought different because from the start he felt different. He was born in 1955 in San Francisco to a Syrian graduate student and his U.S. girlfriend, who placed him for adoption. He was raised by Paul and Clara Jobs—Paul was a machinist; Clara was an accountant. Jobs was only 21 in 1976 when he started Apple with his buddy Steve ("Woz") Wozniak, a brilliant engineer whose career was later sidelined by a plane crash. Jobs had spent one unhappy semester and a few months more "dropping in" on classes at Reed College in Portland, Ore. He'd made a pilgrimage to India and dabbled with psychedelic drugs and primal-scream therapy.

Downtime *Jobs relaxes at home in Palo Alto in 2004. When he unveiled the first Macintosh in 1984, he called it "insanely great," a phrase that came to define his hopes for Apple*

Jobs revolutionized industries every few years with stunning regularity: computers, movies, music, phones

The two Steves' first major breakthrough, the Apple II in 1977, sported both ease of use and stylish case design: the first stirrings of Jobs' keen consumer instincts. It was a hit, but more was to come. In 1979 Jobs visited Xerox's PARC research lab in Palo Alto, Calif., where he saw an experimental computer with a graphical user interface and a mouse. For him, it was a vision of the future. PARC's ideas showed up in 1984 in the shape of the Macintosh, the first computer to harness these then highly innovative and now ubiquitous tools.

As a manager, Jobs was tough, dismissive, abrasive. Among the people whose buttons he pushed was Apple's president, John Sculley, formerly the CEO of Pepsi, whom Jobs had lured to his company. Frustrated with the know-it-all Jobs, Sculley and the Apple board trimmed his wings; he left the company in 1985. He used his Apple millions to found NeXT, which made sleek, expensive computers that didn't sell but whose software eventually became the soul of many Apple products.

For years, Jobs' second post-Apple venture, Pixar, struggled, but soon its computer-generated cartoons started winning Oscars. When Pixar's 1995 *Toy Story* became the year's top-grossing movie, it gave Jobs his first unqualified success in a decade. He later called the NeXT-Pixar years "one of the most creative periods of my life." It was also the time when he started a family. He married Laurene Powell in 1991; by 1998 they were the parents of a son and two daughters.

Meanwhile, sans Jobs, Apple was failing. Seeking a new start, CEO Gil Amelio bought NeXT and invited Jobs to return to the company in 1997. Within months, Jobs had orchestrated Amelio's departure and was back at the helm. He now staged the greatest comeback in the history of business, as Apple rolled out one triumphant product after another. In 1998 the company released the all-in-one iMac, which came in a translucent candy-colored case. In May 2001, the first Apple Store opened. Later that year came the iPod music player: Apple was now in the consumer-electronics business.

When Apple unveiled the iTunes Music Store to feed its iPods in 2003, it revolutionized the music business. In 2007 came the iPhone, a powerful personal computer that fit in your pocket, and whose touchscreen interface instantly made every other smartphone on the market look like an antique. In 2010 Jobs introduced the iPad, the first tablet computer to become a hit with the public. But even as Apple soared, Jobs' health failed. In 2004 he was given a diagnosis of pancreatic cancer; in 2009 he received a liver transplant. He resigned as Apple's CEO on Aug. 24, 2011, only six weeks before he died at 56.

It's a rule of thumb in the world of technology that you get to revolutionize one industry at most, but Jobs did so every few years with stunning regularity: computers, movies, music, phones. He built some of the greatest tools for creativity and self-expression that humanity has ever seen. Their perfection suggests both a deep empathy with others and also a raging aggression toward them: he would make things so perfect that we could not refuse them. He wanted the rest of us to live our own lives as fully and richly as he did, and he was going to make absolutely sure we did, whether we liked it or not.

—By Lev Grossman and Harry McCracken

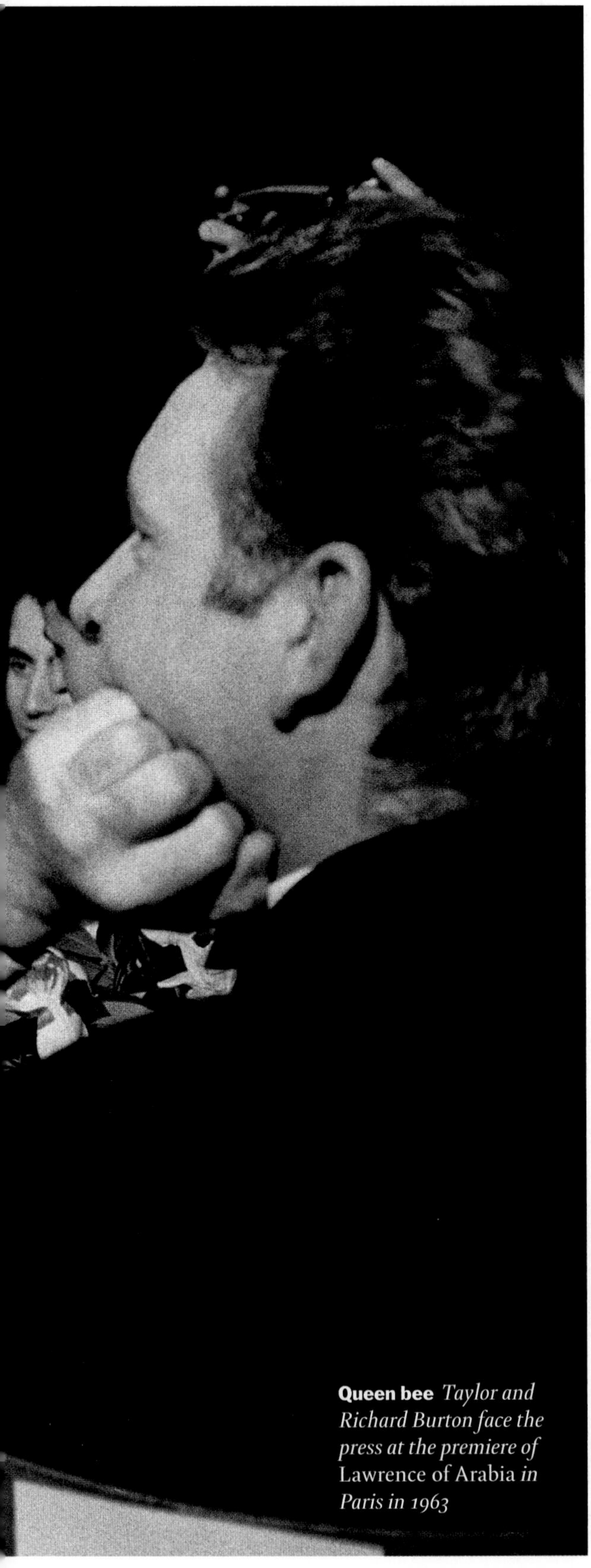

Queen bee *Taylor and Richard Burton face the press at the premiere of* Lawrence of Arabia *in Paris in 1963*

REPORTERS ASSOCIES/GAMMA-RAPHO VIA GETTY IMAGES

Elizabeth Taylor

To the end, she was Hollywood royalty

ELIZABETH ROSEMUND TAYLOR WAS BORN in 1932 in London to Francis Taylor, an American art dealer living there, and his wife Sara, who had acted on Broadway under the name Sara Sothern and retired after she married. When war arrived in Britain, the Taylors immigrated to California, where Sara had notions of finding for her daughter the stardom that had eluded her. At 10, Elizabeth was fighting for screen space with Carl ("Alfalfa") Switzer in a Universal programmer called *There's One Born Every Minute.* She seems mesmerized by the camera; she practically stares a hole through the lens. Her intensity was lost on Universal production boss Edward Muhl, who terminated her contract with this pungent critique: "She can't sing, she can't dance, she can't perform."

Maybe not. Yet from a few years after MGM signed her in 1943 to the end of her contract in the early 1960s and beyond, Taylor was routinely called the world's most beautiful woman. The label stuck to her like a price tag on the 33.19-carat Krupp diamond, one of her many famous gems. It set a tab on her allure—and on the most public of Hollywood's "private lives"—while obscuring her value as an actress and an enduring symbol of American moviemaking. Many talented tyros had been bred in the studio hothouse. But in the 1940s, none came to flower so luxuriantly; in the '50s, none found so bracing a challenge in Hollywood's search for artistic maturity; and in the '60s, when the system collapsed, none survived it so craftily as Taylor did.

The marriage records, tabulating her eight weddings and seven divorces, would list her as Elizabeth Taylor Hilton Wilding Todd Fisher Burton Burton Warner Fortensky. The AIDS patients she helped with her brave, exhaustive work raising millions of dollars for treatment of the disease might call her St. Elizabeth, or Mom. But to generations of film fans and paparazzi, from her MGM debut at age 11 to her death of congestive heart failure in Los Angeles on March 23 at 79, she was simply Liz. Indomitable and irreplaceable, embodying glamour, excess and beguilement, she was *the* Hollywood star.

—*Richard Corliss*

Betty Ford

She won our hearts by shedding light on life's darker corners

TRANSPARENCY IS NOT THE NORMAL FIRST Lady format: life in the White House means trying to keep your sanity, keep your husband grounded and keep out of trouble. This is always easier to manage as a porcelain figurine propped at the President's side than as a living, breathing, conspicuously imperfect and opinionated partner who doesn't try to hide her weaknesses. Betty Ford was by no means the first strong and influential First Lady, but she was the first to take her personal power public in ways that changed the role and the country at the same time.

She was perfectly suited to her time—29 months in the White House, during which America was catching its breath and checking its pulse to see if basic institutions and assumptions could survive the shock of the Nixon presidency. Her husband Jerry loved her fizzy candor, her firm commitment when she believed in something and her refusal to pretend when she didn't. She wore a mood ring, but that was redundant; she wasn't one to hide an attitude anyway, any more than she'd hide how much her psychiatrist had helped her or what she thought of her children's sex lives or which of her breasts was removed by doctors when she got cancer. So as the U.S. wrestled with the role it wanted women to play, she marched with Betty Friedan in support of the Equal Rights Amendment. As the political stars realigned for a generation around *Roe,* she called the court's abortion ruling "a great, great decision." As the trauma of Vietnam lingered, she discussed amnesty for draft dodgers.

When after seven weeks in the White House she discovered the cancer, she bared her pain in public, discussing her treatment, including a radical mastectomy, bluntly and in detail. But her discomfort was a price she willingly paid; millions of women began performing self-exams, going for screenings—and telling Ford she had saved their lives by helping them detect cancer early. In much the same way, she later made public her battle with alcoholism and prescription drug dependency. Thanks to the clinic she founded in California, her very name became synonymous with intensive, serious rehabiltative treatment for a disease that can hit anyone—a disease, she noted, not loose morals or lack of willpower. When she died Friday, July 8, at age 93, America lost one of its most unlikely and unmatched healers.

—*Nancy Gibbs*

Irrepressible *The First Lady, a professional dancer in her youth, cuts a rug on the Cabinet Room table in 1977, right. Below left, with husband Gerald Ford after her breast cancer surgery in 1974; below right, she sports an ERA pin in 1975*

RIGHT: DAVID HUME KENNERLY—COURTESY GERALD R. FORD LIBRARY; LEFT, FROM LEFT: DAVID HUME KENNERLY—COURTESY GERALD R. FORD LIBRARY; KARL SCHUMACHER—COURTESY GERALD R. FORD LIBRARY

Cautious steward *Christopher in later years. He was the chief U.S. negotiator with Iran during the hostage crisis of 1979-80*

Warren Christopher

Former President Bill Clinton remembers his first Secretary of State

WARREN CHRISTOPHER, WHO DIED MARCH 18 at 85, headed my vice-presidential search committee and recommended Al Gore. As the leader of my presidential transition team, he oversaw the creation of the talented, dedicated and diverse group that was crucial to the prosperity the U.S. enjoyed in the 1990s. Then he became Secretary of State. Chris had the lowest ego-to-accomplishment ratio of any public servant I've ever worked with. That made him easy to underestimate. But all Americans should be grateful that he possessed the stamina, steel and judgment to accomplish things that were truly extraordinary.

As our first post–cold war Secretary of State, he faithfully and effectively advanced U.S. interests and values: ending the war in Bosnia and forging the Dayton peace accords; relentlessly moving the Middle East peace process forward; reducing the nuclear threat on the Korean peninsula; supporting security cooperation with Russia; expanding NATO; increasing our investments in Africa and partnerships with Asian nations; championing human rights; and alerting the public to the danger of global warming. Christopher's tireless efforts, keen judgment and old-fashioned patriotism helped the U.S. meet the challenges of the post–cold war world. I was honored by his service and enriched by his friendship.

—*Bill Clinton*

RINGO CHIU—ZUMAPRESS.COM

Visiting dignitary *Young Turkish students surround Shriver, then Peace Corps director, on a world tour in 1964*

Sargent Shriver

The passionate liberal was the Great Society's greatest visionary

WHEN AGING LIBERALS AND YOUNG progressives think longingly of Camelot and the Great Society, they usually have a mental picture of the Kennedy brothers. But perhaps the purest representative of that era of Big Government idealism was a brother-in-law, Sargent Shriver, who died on Jan. 18 at a hospital in Maryland at age 95.

Hardly a starry-eyed program was launched in the 1960s without Shriver's imprint. He took John F. Kennedy's campaign promise of a volunteer youth corps and created the Peace Corps, serving as its first director. After J.F.K.'s death, Shriver put his stamp on Lyndon Johnson's Great Society. As first director of the Office of Economic Opportunity, he launched the VISTA program, the Job Corps, Head Start, the Community Action Program and other initiatives in the War on Poverty.

That many of these programs promised far more than they delivered was a contributing factor in the decline of liberalism after 1968. Yet the best of his ideas—including Head Start and the Peace Corps—have endured. And in the private sector, he was a key figure in the global growth of his late wife Eunice Kennedy Shriver's great legacy, the Special Olympics, which has changed the way people with disabilities are treated and valued. For liberals, Shriver was the genuine article.

—David Von Drehle

PAUL CONKLIN—PIX INC.—TIME LIFE PICTURES

Grandeur in graffiti *Twombly poses in 2005 with his 1994 painting* Untitled (Say Goodbye, Catullus, to the Shores of Asia Minor)

Cy Twombly

The painter embraced primitive techniques to meld past and present

THE ARTIST CY TWOMBLY SOUGHT TO SUMmon a spirit of the classical past in a visual language that was both resolutely of the here and now and so "primitive"—scribbles, loops, scratches and the doodles of graffiti—that it seemed to stand outside of time altogether. In a way, he was born into nostalgia for a vanished past, in Lexington, Va., amid the faded glories of the Old South. In 1957 he relocated to Italy, another place shattered by war and inclined to look longingly back on lost grandeur. He sifted the rubble of postwar Europe to find a usable model in graffiti—crude marks that seemed as old as antiquity and in touch with the hidden currents of human affairs. Borrowing from the Surrealists, he experimented with sketching in the dark; for a time he forced himself to draw with his left hand. In his work, hectic scribbles and smudges of color might share the canvas with a crudely drawn phrase that harked back to the classical world but always dimly, a fading signal, the remnant of a broken order, the sweaty Dionysian scrimmage rather than the white marble realm of Apollo.

His art was slow to find favor at home: a Manhattan gallery show in 1964 got a calamitous critical reaction. But in the 1980s a new generation of Neo-Expressionist painters claimed him as a precursor, and in his last decades, Twombly became one of the most honored and sought-after American artists. He died at 83 on July 5.

—*Richard Lacayo*

MICHAEL STRAVATO—THE NEW YORK TIMES—REDUX PICTURES

Amy Winehouse

She lived fast and died young. Any questions?

HER DEATH, SADLY, came as no surprise. With stints in rehab, court appearances, a troubled marriage and a canceled June 2011 tour due to a shambolic performance in Serbia, where she appeared too drunk to perform, British retro-soul singer Amy Winehouse had problems that were there for all to see. In fact, she had parlayed those problems into fame and fortune: in her best-known song, *Rehab,* she defied those who urged her to walk the path of moderation. Instead, Winehouse followed William Blake's directive: "The road of excess leads to the palace of wisdom." It also led to the discovery of her dead body in her London home on July 23. On Oct. 26, a coroner reported that the 27-year-old's demise was a "death by misadventure," saying an autopsy showed the singer's blood-alcohol level was more than four times the legal limit for drunk driving in Britain. No illegal drugs were detected.

Winehouse stumbled upon a musical career as a 16-year-old when her demo tape landed in the hands of her friend, soul singer Tyla James, who helped her secure a record deal. In 2003 she released her first CD, *Frank,* to critical acclaim and moderate success. Her 2006 follow-up, *Back to Black,* brought her international fame. Channeling the dark, jazzy, soulful styles of eras past, she wowed audiences the world over. Sadly, we will never know if there was an Act II within her.

DENNY RENSHAW—CORBIS OUTLINE

Joe Frazier

"Smokin' Joe" earned his fame as Muhammad Ali's toughest rival

JOE FRAZIER GREW UP IN BEAUFORT, S.C., where he was raised in a four-room shack on a farm and threw his first punches against a feed bag stuffed with rags, hung from an oak tree. Jim Crow sent Frazier fleeing from South Carolina; the teenager hitchhiked to Charleston and, as he said, "caught the first thing smokin' that was goin' north." Frazier settled in Philadelphia, where he took a job as a butcher in a kosher slaughterhouse. He caught the eye of a fight manager at a local Police Athletic League, and lost only one of his amateur fights, to Buster Mathis at the trials for the 1964 Olympics. Mathis got hurt, however, and the trip to the Tokyo Games fell to Frazier. Despite fighting his final match with a broken thumb, Frazier came home from Japan wearing the heavyweight gold medal.

Frazier turned pro in 1965. With Muhammad Ali stripped of his boxing license owing to his refusal to serve in Vietnam, Frazier soared through the heavyweight ranks and won the world title in 1970, the year Ali returned to the ring. Their first face-off—the "Fight of the Century"—came on March 8, 1971. Frazier triumphed in that 15-round slugfest on a decision, but Ali beat him in the epic 1975 "Thrilla in Manila" brawl, when Joe's trainer stopped the fight in the 14th round. Frazier lost his last battle, against cancer, in November at 67, long after he won a place in the pantheon of boxing greats.

AL BELLO—GETTY IMAGES

Pundit's perch *Rooney stares down the camera in 2010 at his office at* 60 Minutes, *his longtime bully pulpit*

TODD PLITT—CONTOUR BY GETTY IMAGES

Andy Rooney

The cranky curmudgeon of *60 Minutes* was beset, bothered—and beloved

THE GLORIOUSLY GRUMPY COMMENTATOR first sat down behind his desk on the CBS Sunday-night newsmagazine show *60 Minutes* on July 2, 1978. It was a seat that would launch him to fame as a cultural icon. From his first commentary to his very last, 33 years later, Andy Rooney played the part of the Everyman, speaking his mind frankly on subjects as haughty as the existence of God and as mundane as wristwatches. He announced his retirement during his 1,097th broadcast on Oct. 2, 2011. Only a month later, the 92-year-old died after complications from minor surgery, fulfilling a prediction he had made to a former colleague. "He told me when he stopped working he probably would die," said Mika Brzezinski, co-host of MSNBC early show *Morning Joe*. "He loved his job."

"I probably haven't said anything here that you didn't already know or have already thought," Rooney noted on his final broadcast. But indeed that's what Rooney was so good at: evaluating the common annoyances of society at such a deep level that it brought clarity and fresh understanding to everyday thoughts.

Said Rooney's longtime colleague Morley Safer: "Underneath that gruff exterior was a prickly interior ... and deeper down was a sweet and gentle man, a patriot with a love of all things American, like good bourbon, and a delicious hatred for prejudice and hypocrisy."

Dan Wheldon

Race-car drivers routinely risk their lives. But fatalities are relatively rare. So when reigning Indy 500 champ Dan Wheldon died on Oct. 16 in a fiery 15-car pileup at the Las Vegas Motor Speedway, racing fans were stunned. Wheldon, 33, who grew up driving go-karts in England, died of blunt head trauma. The popular Briton left behind a wife, two young children—and serious concerns about the safety of his sport.

Before the race, many drivers had warned that banked ovals like the Vegas course were more suited to slower, sturdier NASCAR vehicles than to roofless Indy cars that race on road and street tracks. As four-time series champ Dario Franchitti put it, "I said before we even tested here that this was not a suitable track for us." Wheldon's death proved he was right.

Clarence Clemons

They called him the Big Man. For four decades, the 6-ft. 4-in. tenor saxophonist, who died June 18 at 69, played at the right hand of the Boss, Bruce Springsteen. Clemons' and Springsteen's first meeting serves as the band's origin myth. On a stormy night in 1971, Clemons entered a bar in Asbury Park, N.J., where Springsteen was playing. A gust of wind blew the door from its hinges, and Clemons asked if he could join the set. For the next 30 or so years, the two were inseparable onstage, dancing, spinning, jumping, bridging a nation's long-standing racial divides through the healing ministry of music.

Peter Falk

An average-Joe hero, Peter Falk embodied the best of us on our worst day. His defining role was TV's Lieut. Columbo, who, for 30 years, taught snooty murderers that, however crafty they thought they were, he was smarter. But Falk, who died on June 23 at 83, was also a significant figure in cinema. He spanned the gulf between mainstream movies (like *The In-Laws*) and indie movies (notably the semi-improvised dramas of John Cassavetes) with the ease of a Colossus navigating a mud puddle. Blessed with a crinkly face that viewers found hard not to smile back at, he had one of the great loopy stares in movie history, courtesy of a glass eye, a trophy from a childhood disease. And just one more thing: he was magnificent in *The Princess Bride*.

TOP: CBS PHOTO ARCHIVES—GETTY IMAGES; MIDDLE: BROOKE ISMACH—ZUMAPRESS.COM; BOTTOM: DEBORAH FEINGOLD—CORBIS

Geraldine Ferraro

As Democrat Walter Mondale's running mate in 1984, the three-time Representative from New York was the first woman (and first Italian American) to be part of a major party's presidential ticket. Though she was unfamiliar to most Americans, Geraldine Ferraro had the qualifications for the job. Respected in Congress, she was a key player in the formulation of the Democratic Party's platform and convention rules.

Her backstory too was bracing. The daughter of Italian immigrants, Ferraro pursued a law career when the profession was dominated by men (she was one of two women in her graduating class). As assistant District Attorney in Queens County, she was in charge of the Special Victims Bureau, overseeing cases involving child and spousal abuse. Though married, she continued to use her family name, she said, to honor the mother who, after the death of Geraldine's father, had kept the family going. Her nomination electrified the contest, until her wealthy husband's refusal to publish his tax returns let the air out of the balloon. The courageous, outspoken trailblazer died on March 26 at 75, with her place in history secure.

Jack Kevorkian

"My specialty is death," Dr. Jack Kevorkian once told TIME. In the 1980s he began weighing in on the issue that would make him infamous: euthanasia and the plight of the dying. By the time his own end came—on June 3, at 83—the physician was said to have had a role in more than 130 deaths. Many of them came about through use of the Thanatron, the infamous "suicide machine" he rigged to let his patients self-administer lethal levels of narcotics.

In 1999, after Kevorkian had deftly avoided criminal responsibility in several cases, he was convicted of second-degree murder when video surfaced of him administering a deadly dose. Eight years later, he was paroled; after a quiet period he resumed his crusade, pushing his cause vigorously but never again assisting in suicides.

Though detractors continued to decry his methods, Kevorkian remained confident in his quest. "It's unstoppable," he told TIME. "It may not be in my lifetime, but my opponents are going to lose. There's a lot of human misery out there."

FROM LEFT: GLOBE PHOTOS—ZUMAPRESS.COM; JEFF KOWALSKY—ZUMA PRESS—CORBIS

Jerry Leiber

Jerry Leiber and Mike Stoller *were* rock 'n' roll. They wrote the best primal rock songs, anyway: rhythm-and-blues stompers and every musical genre in between and beyond. *Hound Dog, Jailhouse Rock, Kansas City, Love Potion No. 9, There Goes My Baby,* dozens of rude immortals. Ballads too: *Stand By Me, On Broadway* and (Leiber's words, Phil Spector's melody) *Spanish Harlem.* L&S wrote and produced the Coasters' run of comedy smashes (*Yakety Yak, Charlie Brown*); produced the Drifters' catalog of gorgeous love songs; godfathered Spector, Carole King and the other gifted Brill Building brats; and wrote and produced the Peggy Lee anthems *I Am Woman* and *Is That All There Is?* Leiber, at right above, and Stoller were inducted into the Rock and Roll Hall of Fame in 1987, its second year. All we can think of is, Why the wait?

The live wire to Stoller's steady ground wire, the young Jerome Leiber was, like Stoller, a Jewish boy who loved the blues. Stoller was the composer, running dozens of cunning variations on the traditional 12-bar blues; Leiber wrote the words that never stopped resonating in the ears of generations of arrested teens. The two, born six weeks apart in 1933, were teenagers themselves when they met in Los Angeles in 1950: Stoller, a Long Island transplant, was a first-year student at L.A. City College; Leiber, from Baltimore, had worked in a record store while still a senior in high school. "Red-hot songs were born on the black streets of Baltimore," he recalled in the oral history *Hound Dog: The Leiber & Stoller Autobiography.* The duo scored their first hits before they were 20 and kept at it for 60 years. Jerry Leiber died on Aug. 22. The primal poet of rock was 78.

—Richard Corliss

Jack LaLanne

Before Richard Simmons, there was Jack LaLanne. Clad in his trademark shiny jumpsuits, LaLanne was among the first fitness gurus to exhort Americans to get off the couch and get active. He led by example, exercising every day until his death on Jan. 23 at age 96.

Helming one of the first workout shows on TV, LaLanne encouraged viewers by saying, "Come on, now, girls. We're going to work on"—he'd pat his rear—"reducing the old back porch." A great salesman and avid promoter of the fit lifestyle, he regularly performed stunts during his 60s to prove that physical fitness was ageless. Even after having heart surgery in his '90s, he refused to let his mortality slow him down. "I can't afford to die," he said. "It would wreck my image." Not to worry, Jack. Your personality and your legacy will live on.

—Alice Park

GEORGE ROSE—GETTY IMAGES (2)

Sidney Lumet

For a half-century, Sidney Lumet was the primary apostle of streetwise cinema, the torch-bearer of ground-glass realism and the ultimate chronicler of New York City in all its agita and chutzpah. A fat fistful of his New York films—*12 Angry Men, The Pawnbroker, Serpico, Dog Day Afternoon, Network, Prince of the City*—could serve as a time capsule of the American metropolis in its violent grandeur, its cunning, desperation and raw wit. Let Woody Allen profile the upper middle class of neurotic literati; Lumet's films were more like ransom notes, third-degree confessions, anguished screams through the bars of a high-rise window, as in his *Network:* "I'm as mad as hell, and I'm not going to take this any more."

As driven, aggressive and purposeful as any of his film protagonists, Lumet directed 43 feature films, starting with his 1957 debut, *12 Angry Men.* Nominated four times for the Best Director Oscar, and receiving an honorary Academy Award in 2005, Lumet finally ran out of stories, clout and (the last to go) boundless creative energy. He died April 9, at 86, at his Manhattan home.

Lawrence Eagleburger

The only career foreign service officer ever to be named Secretary of State, Lawrence Eagleburger enjoyed a long and storied career as an American diplomat that began in the 1950s. He was the quiet (and sometimes not so quiet) guiding force behind several decades of politically appointed Secretaries of State. He served Democrats as well as Republicans, from Eisenhower to Bush 1, and formed a particularly strong partnership with Henry Kissinger during the Nixon era. He was ideologically moderate, ruthlessly hard-headed about American interests and unusually effective behind the scenes, from pushing visionary ideas through the often sluggish back offices of the State Department to doing the dirty work that his diplomatic superiors chose to avoid. He died at 80 on June 4.

Lanford Wilson

In a period when directors, actors and revivals dominated the theater, Lanford Wilson emerged as a fresh and innovative playwright. He helped create the off-off-Broadway movement, was among the first to tackle issues of gay identity openly onstage, co-founded the influential Circle Repertory Company and wrote works that were hits in their day and promise to continue to hold the stage for decades to come.

Emerging from the small town of Lebanon, Mo., Wilson began writing plays in Chicago and arrived in New York City just as the 1960s were achieving escape velocity. Early works *Balm in Gilead* (directed by longtime collaborator Marshall Mason) and *The Rimers of Eldritch* were well received, paving the way for his best plays, *The Hot l Baltimore* (1973), which became a short-lived TV series; the mainstream Broadway hit *Fifth of July* (1978); the Pulitzer-prizewinning *Talley's Folly* (1979), which, like several of Wilson's plays, was set in his hometown; and *Burn This* (1987), a rueful comedy of modern manners that starred an incendiary young John Malkovich. Wilson, 73, died on March 24.

TOP: SAM FALK—THE NEW YORK TIMES—REDUX PICTURES; BOTTOM, LEFT TO RIGHT: STEFAN ZAKLIN—EPA; MARTY REICHENTHAL—AP IMAGES

Arness

James Arness

For 20 years Arness portrayed the upright lawman Matt Dillon on *Gunsmoke,* one of TV's greatest westerns. Arness (brother of the late Peter Graves) was the picture of Western rectitude: with his square jaw and clean-cut looks, he carried the character with a quiet, deliberate strength, aided by his 6-ft. 7-in. frame. With a few words, he conveyed both toughness and empathy. Arness, who died on June 3 at 88, embodied an archetype but made two decades' worth of TV viewers (and more since) feel they knew Matt Dillon as a person.

Seve Ballesteros

Bursting onto the international golf scene in 1976, Ballesteros quickly proceeded to capture the hearts of links fans the world over, with his swashbuckling, swaggering style; he always chose to go for glory (the hole) rather than the safe percentage shot (the green). His approach helped transform the sport, with his fellow players often inspired to play the game in a similar manner. The charismatic Spaniard's exciting ethos also paid off in trophies: in total, he amassed a staggering 87 over his career, including five majors, before his death on May 7 at the early age of 54.

Ballesteros

Mark Hatfield

After serving in the U.S. Navy in World War II, where he was one of the first Americans to enter the ruins of Hiroshima, Hatfield devoted himself to public service. Following two terms as Oregon's governor, the Republican entered the U.S. Senate in 1967 and became a fixture for three decades, chairing the Appropriations Committee for eight years and winning national respect for hewing to his own views when they differed with those of his party. He died on Aug. 7 at 89.

Hatfield

Chris Hondros

His parents were refugees from World War II Europe, and U.S. photojournalist Hondros devoted himself to documenting conflicts around the world, following Robert Capa's famed maxim: "If your pictures aren't good enough, you aren't close enough." Hondros' images appeared frequently in TIME and won numerous international photo awards. On April 20, Hondros was killed in Misrata, Libya, at age 41, by a rocket-propelled grenade. British photojournalist Tim Hetherington also died in the incident.

Hondros

Madame Ngo Dinh Nhu

Born to an aristocratic Hanoi family, Tran Le Xuan was married to the brother of bachelor President Ngo Dinh Diem, and became South Vietnam's unofficial First Lady in the earliest days of the Vietnam conflict. She earned a reputation with U.S. officials for moral zealotry, crusading against adultery, abortion and dance halls. Americans found her as alluring and repellent as the war. "To some she is an Asian Joan of Arc, to others an Oriental Lucrezia Borgia," wrote TIME in 1962. Her enduring nickname, the Dragon Lady, referred to a femme fatale from a popular U.S. comic strip. It's a sobriquet the ferocious Nhu, who died April 24 at 87, no doubt enjoyed.

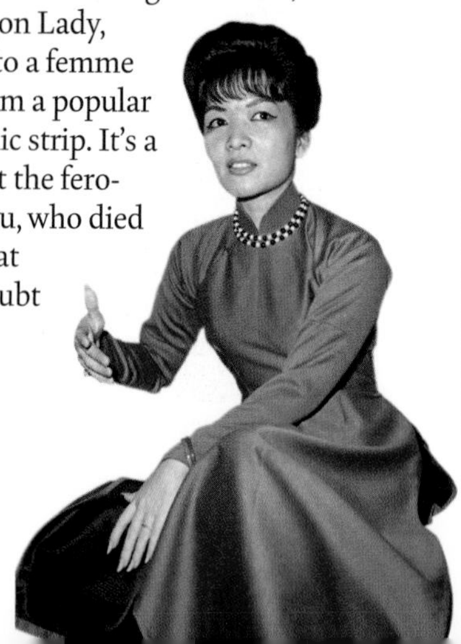

Nhu

ARNESS: CBS PHOTO ARCHIVES—GETTY IMAGES; BALLESTEROS: BOB THOMAS SPORTS PHOTOGRAPHY; HATFIELD: DOUGLAS GRAHAM—ROLL CALL—GETTY IMAGES; HONDROS: GETTY IMAGES; NHU: BETTMANN CORBIS

Robertson

Cliff Robertson

For much of his early career, Robertson created roles on TV and the stage—like Joe Clay in *The Days of Wine and Roses* and Val Xavier in *Orpheus Descending*—only to find himself passed over when the opportunity arose to play them on the big screen. But in 1960, Robertson, who died Sept. 10 at 88, took matters into his own hands. While filming a TV movie about a mentally disabled janitor, Robertson bought the film rights and worked for eight years to bring it to theaters. He won an Oscar for starring in that story's film version, *Charly.* Above, he starred as J.F.K. in *PT-109* in 1963.

Jane Russell

The statuesque brunette rose to fame after Howard Hughes selected her for his 1943 film *The Outlaw,* and controversy followed over the prominence of her cleavage onscreen. The woman Bob Hope once introduced as "the two and only" forged a substantial postwar career in comedies, dramas and musicals before retiring from acting in films full time in 1957. Afterward, she began a family and founded the World Adoption International Agency, which helped find homes for overseas orphans. She died on Feb. 28 at 89.

Russell

George Shearing

Sightless from birth, the pianist first conquered his native Britain, then came to the U.S. in 1947, where TIME hailed his tuneful light jazz in 1950 as "sherbet cold ... [playing] as though he were tapping on tuned icicles." The piano man's charm and feathery, melodic touch kept him at the top of his craft until he retired in 2004. Knighted in 2007, Shearing died Feb. 14 at 91.

Shearing

Duke Snider

In the 1950s, during New York City's golden era of baseball, there were Willie, Mickey and the Duke—the on-field leaders of the city's three ball clubs. Snider, who died Feb. 27 at 84, was a perfectionist on the field who helped lead the Brooklyn Dodgers to their sole championship, in 1955, and became the only player to twice hit four home runs in a World Series.

Snider

Grete Waitz

No. 1173. When she crossed the finish line of the New York City Marathon in 1978, Grete Waitz was nothing more than a bib number. It was, after all, her first marathon. Yet the Norwegian, who died of cancer on April 19 at 57, set a world record that year by running the marathon in 2 hr. 32 min. She went on to win an unprecedented eight more New York City Marathons, became the first female marathoner to break the 2½-hr. mark and won silver in the 1984 Olympics. Back in Norway, she was a humble hero who possessed one of the most recognizable names in her sport—a name that didn't even appear in the original race program back in 1978.

Waitz

INDEX